W9-CBN-556

Techniques of Mediation in Labor Disputes

by Walter A. Maggiolo

1971
OCEANA PUBLICATIONS, INC.
Dobbs Ferry, New York

Library of Congress Cataloging in Publication Data

Maggiolo, Walter A   1908-
    Techniques of mediation in labor disputes.
    Bibliography: p.
    1. Mediation and conciliation, Industrial--U.S.
2. Mediation and conciliation, Industrial.
I. Title.
HD5504.A3M24   331.89'14   70-166000
ISBN 0-379-00112-8

The views expressed herein are those of the author and not necessarily those of the Federal Mediation and Conciliation Service.

To

Henry - an outstanding mediator

and a source of inspiration.

CONTENTS

PREFACE

The task of the mediator has seldom been an enviable one. Mercutio, unable to achieve any sort of accommodation between the warring Montagues and Capulets, could only exclaim in exasperation, "A plague o' both your houses."

But Mercutio was not a trained mediator, nor was mediation in his time the highly developed art that it is today. To reach its full potential, mediation had to wait until the advent of collective bargaining. Attempts at mediating labor disputes were tried in the late 19th century in the United States and even earlier in England . But really effective efforts in this country date from the establishment of the Department of Labor in 1913 and the subsequent appointment of "commissioners of conciliation," reconstituted in 1947 as the Federal Mediation and Conciliation Service we know today.

Walter Maggiolo's career spans almost the entire lifetime of serious mediation efforts in this country. During that career he has participated in the settlement of hundreds of labor disputes covering the whole spectrum of business and industry. And during that career he has picked up a wealth of skill and knowledge along the way.

This book is a distillation of that skill and knowledge. Readers will discover that mediation is indeed an art, an art demanding the utmost in human relations skills.

It is also becoming an increasingly important art. The need for skilled mediators in our society is increasing. The recent rapid expansion of collective bargaining into the public sector is creating a rising demand for mediation services at all levels--

Federal, State, and local. Nor do we see any diminution of that demand in the years ahead. Government service, particularly in the States and local communities, is one of the greatest anticipated growth areas of this decade.

But mediation is no field for the untrained or even for the merely well-intentioned. It demands a high degree of expertise in many fields, particularly in the elusive but all-important field of interpersonal relations. Mr. Maggiolo's book deals incisively with the whys and wherefores of mediation and the role of the mediator. But, more important than that, it is a "how to" book. It is replete with suggestions and advice on how to handle mediation situations--the thousand and one impasses, disagreements, traps, and problems with which the mediator finds himself confronted.

It is a book for the student and practitioner. It could only have been written by a man who has not only had long experience in actual mediation but who has trained others in this difficult art.

Mr. Maggiolo is such a man, and he has written a very useful and altogether commendable book.

J.D. HODGSON
Secretary of Labor

1 THE PHILOSOPHY OF MEDIATION

To evaluate properly the role of mediation in the field of labor-management relations, it must be cast in a much broader setting. It should be assessed in the light of some of the basic concepts upon which our democratic society has been founded.

Our society is fundamentally a "meeting-of-minds" civilization. Our whole way of life is predicated on the principle that while the individual members of our society may have varying economic, political and social backgrounds and consequently divergent viewpoints, when occasion demands, they can and must subordinate and accommodate their self interest to the common good. As members of a democratic society, each individual group although starting from apparently widely divergent positions, can by the process of reasoning, utilization of the normal avenues of communication, discussion, judicious use of constructive compromise and recognition of the dignity of human ideas arrive at a "meeting of minds" and go down the road together toward a common objective--the overriding public welfare. Conflict is thus supplanted by cooperation.

Our society is also predicated on the principle of voluntarism as opposed to compulsion. Duties as well as rights flow out of the social relationship. The primary burden of carrying out the purpose of the society properly is upon the individual members or groups rather than the governing power. To the extent that the component individuals voluntarily assume and exercise their individual responsibilities as members of the society to resolve their own political, economic and social differences, a democracy is strengthened and flourishes.

Further, there is an inter-relationship between all group economic actions and the common welfare. This relationship is effectuated in our democratic society through a recognition that private economic rights may not be exercised in a manner which will override the paramount public interest of the society as a whole.

Consistent with these basic principles, we have evolved our national policy by defining relative responsibilities for maintaining industrial peace.

This policy is not new. Its roots may be found in the Labor Board of World War I, in the 1918 recommendations of the War Labor Conference Board, in Section 7(a) of the N.I.R.A. and in Section 502 of the National Production Act. It is implicit in the spirit and letter of the Wagner Act and the Labor Management Relations Act, 1947.

Essentially, this national policy charges both labor and management with the primary responsibility of making collective bargaining work, and through acceptance of this responsibility, to seek amicable solutions to their labor disputes. In turn, the government has the responsibility of defining the base lines within which justice demands that the parties confine themselves and, as assistance, to the parties, making available to them full and adequate facilities for conciliation and mediation.

It is not the responsibility of this government, except in periods of emergency, to dictate to the parties the terms of their collective bargaining contract. This is as it should be. A basic tenet of a free society is that subsidiary groups or individuals within it should not compel the governing body to undertake functions which they themselves should perform.

Mediation espouses and implements these fundamental social doctrines. Its very purpose is to assist the parties to exercise their baisc responsibility to maintain industrial peace. Further, it is an entirely voluntary process which permits the parties to negotiate their own agreement free from government compulsion or dictation.

2 TECHNIQUES OF SETTLING LABOR DISPUTES

In the United States today, there are four basic techniques used for the settlement of labor disputes--arbitration, fact-finding, mediation and collective bargaining.

Collective Bargaining

Collective bargaining has been described as the process by which representatives of a company and representatives of its employees meet to discuss and negotiate the various phases of their relationship, which have been declared to be proper subject matters of bargaining, with the objective of arriving at a mutually acceptable labor agreement.

An agreement arrived at by successful collective bargaining without the use of any substitute, aid or adjunct is the most desirable method of settlement of any labor dispute.

If the settlement is cast with a consciousness of the public interest, an agreement arrived at through voluntary collective bargaining reflects the full assumption of the basic responsibility for the maintenance of industrial peace by the parties themselves.

Arbitration

Arbitration, in the context of labor disputes, has been described as the submission of a dispute to a neutral or a group of neutrals whose function is to conduct a hearing and render a judgment (termed an award) which is binding upon the parties.

Arbitration can be either compulsory or voluntary. Arbitration is compulsory if the submission of the dispute to the neutral

3

is based not on the consent, expressed or implied, of the parties but rather an administrative or legal compulsion or direction.

In the United States today, the only instances of compulsory arbitration are found in some state statutes relating to public utilities or "industries affected with a public interest". In such states,[1] the legislature having restricted or prohibited the right to strike realized the necessity for some machinery to adjust labor disputes arising in these industries. Compulsory arbitration was the selected process.

Arbitration is voluntary when the submission to the neutral is based on the consent, expressed or implied, of the parties. This is the most widely used arbitration method. It is most prevalent as the terminal point of the grievance procedure provisions of collective bargaining contracts.

Arbitration is termed by many as a substitute for collective bargaining. However, most professional arbitrators insist that it is merely an extension of collective bargaining.

Types of Arbitration

There are three basic types of arbitration: permanent or impartial chairman, tripartite and ad hoc.

A number of collective bargaining contracts name one individual as the "permanent" or impartial chairman who has been selected by the parties to act as arbitrator for all disputes arising under the existing contract. His term of office expires coincidental with the expiration of the contract. Normally his compensation is based on a retainer plus a per diem which is shared by both parties.

Those who espouse this type of arbitration allege that such a person will become thoroughly versed in the terms of the collective bargaining contract and the application of those provisions in the particular company involved and thus assure consistency and uniformity in the awards rendered on the disputes which arise during the contract term. They further state that this type of arbitration avoids necessity of "educating" an arbitrator each time

---

[1] Examples of such states are Florida, Indiana, Wisconsin and Nebraska. cf Bus Employees v. Wisconsin Board, 340 U.S. 383; Amalgamated Association v. Missouri, 374 U.S. 74.

4

a dispute arises as to the collective bargaining contract provisions and plant practices.

A variation of the "permanent" arbitrator type found in some contracts is the naming of three or more arbitrators. Such arbitrators serve on a rotating basis for the duration of the contract.

In the tripartite type, each party to the collective bargaining agreement selects his own representative on the arbitration panel. The two so selected then pick the neutral chairman. The three then hear and determine disputes arising under the contract as a panel. Normally the vote of the majority determines the disposition of the issue presented.

The proponents of this type of arbitration allege that this method assures that each party's viewpoint will be considered not only at the hearing but also when the panel is deliberating its award.

If this method is chosen, care must be taken to make provision for the selection of the neutral in the event the two appointees are unable to agree. The most practical way of breaking such an impasse is to provide in the collective bargaining agreement that the two appointees must agree on the neutral within a limited time period. Upon failure to do so, provision should be made that such neutral will be selected by an outside agency--either the Federal Mediation and Conciliation Service or the American Arbitration Association.

Under the ad hoc type, the arbitrators are selected on a case-by-case basis. Generally speaking, the practice is to provide that if the parties fail to agree on an arbitrator within a prescribed time period, some agency who maintains an arbitration roster will be requested either to submit a panel or to make a direct appointment of a neutral.

Those who advocate this type of arbitration assert that it has a number of advantages over the permanent chairman and the tripartite types. It is stated that one or the other party, or both, may become dissatisfied with the permanent chairman during the contract term but are not in the position to change him until the expiration of the contract which may have one or two more years to run. They also urge that the ad hoc approach is more realistic than the tripartite type. They argue that the arbitrators nominated by each party must of necessity be partisan and consequently the real decision is made by the neutral. Ad hoc arbitration, they

5

say cuts through this sham and additionally assures more expeditious disposition of the grievance.

Obtaining the Services of an Arbitrator

In addition to the Federal Mediation and Conciliation Service and the American Arbitration Association, there are several state agencies which maintain a roster of people who have been selected by the agency as being qualified to handle the arbitration of labor disputes.

Many contracts provide that if the parties are unable to agree on an arbitrator either may request one of the agencies mentioned above to provide them with a panel of available arbitrators. Upon receipt of such a request, unless otherwise specified, the agency will send to each party a panel of seven arbitrators. Accompanying such panel is usually a short biographical sketch of each name appearing thereon. The parties then meet and usually by a system of alternatively striking, arrive at a selection and then advise the agency of the name of the arbitrator selected.

Another practice followed by some is for each to independently indicate opposite the panel member's name their first, second and third choice. Each then transmits to the agency his order of choice. The agency will then compare the two transmissions and appoint as arbitrator the one upon whom there is agreement, or absent an agreement, the arbitrator standing the highest in the order of preference indicated by both parties.

Upon notification of his appointment, the arbitrator has a duty to contact promptly both parties to arrange for a date for the hearing. The proceedings are then conducted under the rules and regulations* prescribed by the appointing agency.

It is important to note that at the point when the agency appoints the arbitrator selected by the parties or, if desired, by direct designation, the arbitrator so selected or designated is not an employee of the appointing agency but an employee of the parties themselves. Consequently, the questions of fee and its collection, dates of hearing, procedures, briefs, stenographic records and

---

* For text of rules and regulations of the Federal Mediation and Conciliation Service and the American Arbitration Association cf Appendix A and B.

6

the like are matters to be decided between the parties and the arbitrator.

Similarly, the merits of the award, its modification or its enforcement must be pursued by the parties. The appointing agency has no authority to review, modify or enforce the arbitrator's award.

As to the per diem fee of arbitrators, most agencies have a suggested fee. Further, as far as the Federal Mediation and Conciliation Service is concerned, each arbitrator listed on its roster must certify to the Service his normal per diem fee. The biographical sketch sent to the parties reflects such per diem charge.

The appointing agency does however, investigate complaints of excessive charges, improper conduct and undue delays in either scheduling hearings or rendition of awards.

Fact-Finding

Fact-finding has been described as the submission of a dispute to a neutral or group of neutrals whose duty it is to conduct hearings, find the facts concerning the dispute and make such findings public. Fact-finding does not necessarily imply any duty of the fact-finding body to make recommendations for the settlement of the dispute.

The theory behind fact-finding is that once the neutral or neutrals have found the facts and made them a matter of public knowledge there will be a marshalling of public opinion. The moral force of such marshalled public opinion will persuade the disputants to change their prior positions and make agreement possible.

Like arbitration, fact-finding can be either compulsory or voluntary. An example of compulsory fact-finding is found in Section 206 of the Labor-Management Relations Act, 1947, as amended, relating to the appointment of boards of inquiry in emergency disputes. A few states such as Missouri have a form of compulsory fact-finding for disputes involving public utilities.

Voluntary fact-finding occurs when the procedure is founded on the consent, expressed or implied, of the parties to the dispute. It has been utilized in disputes involving initial contracts, contract renewals and the adjustment of grievances especially those concerned with incentive or work-load problems. One form of voluntary fact-finding is the agreement by the parties during negotiations to refer certain issues to a committee for further study during the ensuing contract term. Such a procedure when utilized in good faith (and not merely as a device to sweep sticky issues under the carpet) has several desirable objectives. It removes from the emotionally charged negotiating atmosphere issues which can block the successful conclusion of negotiations. It avoids decisions based on expediency and prompted solely by the impending economic crisis. It enables the parties calmly, thoroughly and objectively to delve into the various aspects of the problem and suggest long range approaches to its solution.

Many industrial relations students warn against the indiscriminate use of fact-finding as a labor dispute solving technique. They argue, and with some force and validity, that its potential use must be measured in each case against the background and impact of the dispute on the public. Prescinding from the cases which truly involve the national health and safety, they urge that unless there is present a strong underlying problem of public inconvenience there will be no marshalling of public opinion with its moral persuasive force. They illustrate their point by citing two situations. If a strike is called by the drivers of a major urban or inter-urban transit company, large segments of the working population are immediately affected. Their inability to travel to their place of employment or the bothersome details of arranging alternate methods of transportation are inconveniences which arouse strong and sometimes violent opinions. The findings of a board in this setting can be most efficacious since there will be a quick public opinion response.

The second illustration they offer is a strike involving a small or medium size plant in an industrial community which is not wholly dependent on it. No public convenience is involved. Persons not immediately connected with the dispute would have little interest in any findings of a board. Consequently, there is no marshalling of public opinion, one of the essential ingredients of the dispute settling process.

One of the popular misconceptions about fact-finding is that it necessarily involves the making of recommendations for the settlement of the dispute. No fact-finding board has the inherent

8

right to make such recommendations. In its pure sense, fact-finding confines itself to a public finding of the facts. The power to go the further step of recommendation must be specifically granted to the Board. It can be founded either on the consent of the parties or in the statute creating the board.

An example of pure fact-finding is the one previously cited--the Boards of Inquiry appointed pursuant to Section 206 of the Labor-Management Act, 1947.

Since the recognition of the right of public employees to organize and bargain collectively with their agencies, an increasing amount of state legislatures are adopting statutory procedures for the resolution of this type of dispute. Many of the state statutes provide for a form of fact-finding as a substitute for the right to strike.

In the Federal sector, the Impasse Panel, created by Executive Order 11491, appoints one or more public factfinders to inquire into disputes over which it has assumed jurisdiction. Such factfinders are limited to finding the facts and are prohibited from making recommendations.[2] The right to make recommendations is reserved to the Panel itself.

Under the predecessor order (E. O. 10988), provision was made for "advisory" arbitration.[3] Under that Order, agreements between employee organizations and agencies could provide for advisory arbitration of grievances. Such arbitration had to be advisory in nature with any decision or recommendations:

a) subject to approval of the agency head

b) extend only to the interpretation or application of agreements

c) invoked only with the approval of the individual employee or employees concerned

The cautions are understandable when viewed in the light of the first formal experimentation with employees bargaining in the Federal Sector.

---

[2] Section 2471. 11(a) Rules of the Federal Impasse Panel
[3] Section 8(b), Executive Order 10988

9

"Advisory" arbitration was not a novel concept. For a long period of time, this dispute settling technique was utilized in the private sector particularly in Guild contracts with the wire service companies such as Associated and United Press.

"Advisory" arbitration is really a contradiction in terms since it lacks the finality of true arbitration. Finality is one of the distinguishing attributes between arbitration and fact-finding. "Advisory" arbitration is in reality fact-finding with authority to make recommendations.

Conciliation and Mediation

Generally speaking, mediation or conciliation of a labor dispute has been described as the intercession of an impartial third person in a dispute for the purpose of assisting the parties to resolve their differences voluntarily. The ultimate goal of mediation is to assist disputants to arrive at their own agreement.

Even though the terms conciliation and mediation often are used interchangeably, there is at least a technical distinction between the process of conciliation and mediation.

Conciliation is the more passive role. As is indicated by its latin derivative, it is the act of "gaining good will; to render concordant; to mollify." It involves the bringing of disputing parties together, under circumstances and in an atmosphere most conducive to a discussion of the problem in an objective way for the purpose of seeking a solution to the issue or issues involved. It has been equated to the extension of the "good offices" concept of international law.

Mediation is the more active role. It goes beyond the simple catalytic agent stage. When occasion demands, a mediator interjects himself into the discussions and makes affirmative suggestions and recommendations for developing areas of possible agreement on the issues involved in the dispute.

Both Federal and state mediation statutes, often in the same context, use the two terms synonymously.

In actual practice, the professional mediator when handling a dispute case frequently alternates between the role of a conciliator and that of a mediator. When the discussions are following fruitful paths, he may well adopt the role of the passive chairman. If discussions encounter an apparent roadblock or appear to wander into dead-end lanes, he will resume his role as mediator and by adroit questioning and suggestions either indicate the by-pass or point out the true road.

Most labor disputes present a variety of problems which increase in their complexity in almost direct relationship to the real or assumed economic strength of each party. Attitudes, economic drives and patterns, emotions, breakdown of communications, human relations problems, intra-company and union politics, public relations postures, premature rigidity of positions, personalities--all become enmeshed in the dispute. All too often these obscure the fundamental issues which gave rise to the disagreement.

This is not the uncommon picture which often confronts a mediator when he is called upon to intercede in a labor dispute. He must approach the task before him objectively, calmly and sympathetically.

An immediate prerequisite to his success is the mutual desire of the parties involved to reach agreement. Absent such a desire, no mediator on earth can assist them.

This desire to reach agreement must be a desire to arrive at an equitable accommodation of the conflicting viewpoints of the parties. Each must be willing to be convinced and must be ready to yield to a more reasonable view advanced by the other. A state of mind must exist which has been aptly described as a willingness to accept the less perfect which will lead to agreement and to abandon the perfect which can lead only to continued conflict.

3 FUNDAMENTALS OF EFFECTIVE MEDIATION

There are four fundamental principles for effective mediation:

1. Understanding and appreciation of the problems confronting the parties.

2. Imparting to the parties the fact that the mediator knows and appreciates their problems.

3. Creating doubts in their minds as to the validity of the positions they have assumed with respect to such problems.

4. Suggesting alternative approaches which may facilitate agreement.

The first principle involves a thorough knowledge of the field of labor and industrial relations, awareness of trends and patterns, a working concept of the economics of the industry and particularly the company involved, and an appreciation of any human relations problems which might have precipitated the dispute.

Equally important, the mediator must have a thorough knowledge of the issues which are the immediate causes of the existing impasse and an appreciation of the complexities and dimensions of such problems.

If the mediator does not possess this arsenal of knowledge, he will become a meddler rather than a mediator.

As for the second principle, it is not enough for effective mediation, that the mediator have knowledge and appreciation of

✳ the problems. It is equally important that the parties are made aware of the fact that he does have this knowledge and appreciation. Until this is conveyed to the parties, they will have doubts as to whether he can contribute to the solution of the dispute.

very important The third principle is also essential. Normally, mediation ✳✳ is not utilized until the parties have made good-faith attempts to resolve the dispute without mediation. The fact that the dispute continues is a clear indication that the position one or the other has assumed on a particular issue or issues is a roadblock to agreement. If such position is persisted in, the conflict has little chance of early solution. A mediator's task is then to create doubts as to the validity of that position.

✓ ✳ The mere intercession of a mediator of itself often expedites the agreement-making process. He is the neutral representing the underlying broad public interest. Both parties seek to impress him with the validity of their position, cognizant that their expositions must be stripped of partisan trappings. Their appeal to him must at the very least appear logical rather than emotional. Explanations under such circumstances often creates doubt in the ✳ minds of the parties as to the positions they have assumed.

Beyond the fact of the intercession, the mediator can create doubts by questioning in depth, by bringing into play the broad experience he has acquired and by assisting the parties in evaluating the road ahead in terms of the resultant economic impact.

The fourth principle involves the art of the alternative. Having created such doubts, the mediator must then be prepared to move forward and offer an alternative approach to the problem which may lead to a viable accommodation of the viewpoints of the parties. To do so effectively, the mediator should not only ✳ be knowledgeable but also innovative, imaginative and resourceful. Since a professional mediator's experience in the specific field of collective bargaining is of greater depth than most if not all negotiators for labor or management, he can direct the parties' attention to successful methods for resolution which have been adopted by others. The alternative suggested by the mediator may not be the one finally agreed to by the parties but his suggestion is often designed to open up an approach which can lead to the structuring of the final settlement.

13

4   WHEN SHOULD A MEDIATOR
INTERCEDE IN A DISPUTE

There is a sharp disagreement among the authorities in the field of mediation as to the proper time for a mediator to intercede in a dispute.

One school of thought suggests that the mediator's assistance should be sought in the early stages of negotiations even before an impasse has been reached. The proponents of this thinking assert that such early intercession would enable the mediator to become thoroughly acquainted with the issues and personalities involved and, when roadblocks are reached in their discussions, he would be in a better position to assist the parties to find accommodations. They argue that if the parties wait until an impasse is reached before seeking a mediator's assistance, the negotiations in effect are in a state of suspense until the mediator becomes familiar with the issues and personalities. Until acquainted with these factors, the mediator is not in a position to make meaningful suggestions either as to substance or procedure. They argue that this is time consuming at a point in bargaining when time is of the essence.

In furtherance of this concept, one authority urged mediation agencies to seriously consider appointing "industry mediators." In effect, such agencies would assign a mediator to a particular industry who would have the continuing responsibility to assist that industry in its collective bargaining problems. The writer pointed out that the value of such an "industry mediator" would lie in the fact that he would become thoroughly versed in the industry's problems and their nuances and overtones; he would get to know the parties intimately and with this background be in a position to render valuable assistance. He stated that, apart from the question of intimate knowledge of the industry, such a procedure would avoid the necessity of "educating" new mediators if an ad hoc method of assignment is utilized.

14

With equal vigor, the other school of thought insists that mediation assistance should not be sought or proffered until the parties have exhausted their own efforts and reached an impasse in their direct negotiations. The proponents of this school point out that one of the keystones to free collective bargaining is our national policy with respect to responsibility for maintaining industrial peace. Under that policy, the primary responsibility for industrial peace rests not on the government but on the parties themselves. If the national policy is sound, then they urge intercession before the parties have exhausted their own efforts and negates its basic purpose. Parties should be encouraged to assume their responsibility to resolve their own disputes without the necessity of any governmental intercession or intervention. Any type of intercession before the parties have had an opportunity to exercise self help, they insist, would have the tendency of a shirking of such responsibility no matter what the nature or scope of the dispute may be.

There are inherent difficulties in both approaches. If the mediator intercedes prior to the existence of an impasse, it is difficult to spell out what role, if any, he should play. As a practical matter, it would be difficult, if not impossible, for a mediator in such circumstance to long avoid participating in the discussions. As a result, when the substantial issues emerge later which could be solved by a fresh viewpoint, the effectiveness of the mediator will have been prematurely dissipated.

5 INDUSTRY MEDIATORS

The idea of "industry mediators" has been tested in a number of situations. The United States Conciliation Service (predecessor agency of the Federal Mediation and Conciliation Service) experimented with the industry approach. In 1939-40, as part of its cooperative program with the Advisory Council on National Defense, the U.S. Conciliation Service selected seven of its commissioners to work with what was then considered key defense industries--oil, aviation, manufacturing, machine tools, rubber and chemicals, building construction, shipbuilding and steel. In 1940-41, this was expanded to nineteen.

After a few years' experience, a number of weaknesses became apparent. While certain peripheral benefits were derived from the prolonged exposure to the problems of a particular industry, the industry mediator's effectiveness began to deteriorate for perfectly understandable reasons. Experience has taught that when a mediator is too readily accessible to the parties, there is a tendency on the part of one side or the other to rely on him without any sincere attempt to resolve the dispute by themselves. In addition, there is a serious question as to whether such an industry commissioner becomes less forceful and persuasive because of this more intimate relationship with the parties. Somewhat parallel with this situation is the experience of so-called "permanent arbitrators" or "impartial chairmen".

A later analogous development highlighted the pitfalls of the industry commissioner approach. One of the Service's directors in a speech urged the representatives of labor and management present to seek the assistance of the Service at the very inception of their negotiations. The theme presented was that by such early entry, the mediator could become thoroughly versed in the problems and be in a position better to assist the parties. Soon there-

16

after, a union advised the Service that it had scheduled its first meeting with the company and requested that a mediator be assigned. When contacted, the company, while expressing some doubts, consented. A mediator was assigned. Very early in the negotiations, the parties found themselves in disagreement on a number of very minor contract changes. None of these issues were serious enough to be the basis for a strike or lock-out. Nevertheless, despite his desires, the mediator was placed in a position of suggesting and urging the parties to accept alternative approaches. As the deadline approached and the parties addressed themselves to the more serious issues, the mediator found that his suggestions were falling on deaf ears. He had become too identified with the problems and lost the effectiveness which a fresh approach engenders. Another mediator was assigned to assist the original mediator and a settlement was arrived at based in large measure on the new mediator's suggestions.

The idea of the efficacy of early entrance by the Service was thereafter discouraged.

A more disturbing objection to the "industry" commissioner concept is of course that it is violative of one of the basic fundamentals of our national policy with respect to relative responsibilities for the maintenance of industrial peace, since it inhibits the exercise in the first instance of that responsibility by the parties themselves.

A more practical and better approach would appear to lie somewhere between the two views expressed. A premature entry certainly will invite all of the difficulties outlined above. By the same token, to await until the last moment before inviting the participation of a mediator and expect him, by some miraculous power, to breathe life into the corpse in which rigor mortis has already set in, is to seek the impossible. This has been illustrated by those cases where the parties have delayed until a few hours before the deadline and then sent out an alarm for a mediator. The mediator, in such cases, finds himself propelled into a situation where the parties have assumed fixed positions on often quite involved and complex issues. He has no opportunity to acquaint himself with the personalities involved, the political interplays or the nature and scope of the issues still in dispute. In the emotionally-charged atmosphere normally characteristic of this situation, it is unrealistic and unjust to expect him in the

17

few remaining hours to conjure up through some sort of Divine revelation a "magic formula" which will bring peace and tranquility.

To be most effective, a mediator must have a reasonable time to absorb, evaluate and analyze the issues properly, to appraise the impact of personalities and to explore areas of possible accommodations. It is only after he has had an opportunity to balance all these factors that a mediator can make an effective contribution to the negotiations.

To assure that the mediator's intercession is timely, both parties should keep the assigned mediator fully apprised of the progress (or lack of it) of the negotiations. In addition, they should acquaint him with the dimensions of the major issues. Armed with this information, he should be able to evaluate the status of the negotiations and make a valued judgment as to the best time to intercede. Because of the depth of his experience in this field, great reliance should be placed in him by the parties.

A few unions[4] have adopted internal procedures which assure that their local unions will utilize the assistance of a Federal mediator before resorting to economic action. These internal procedures are usually incorporated either in the International by-laws or procedures which must be adhered to by the local union before the International will authorize strike action and make strike benefits available.

As a general rule, these procedures require the local unions to demonstrate that they have sought and, if available, utilized the services of a Federal mediator prior to strike action.

Such procedures have a dual advantage. From the International's viewpoint, they guard against precipitous strike action by a local before the possibility of settlement through mediation has been explored. Equally important, it buys the time necessary for a representative of the International union to investigate the dispute and participate in the negotiations before any stoppage takes place. From the mediator's viewpoint, it enables him to enter the dispute before economic action has taken place and

---

[4] International Association of Machinists; Oil, Chemical and Atomic Workers International Union; American Federation of Technical Engineers.

before the many new issues, which usually grow out of strike activities, are raised. Further, he is in a position to forestall strike action by seeking an extension if agreement before the deadline does not appear possible.

"Panels" and "Teams" of Mediators

Not infrequently parties to a labor dispute find that a "panel" or "team" of mediators has been assigned to their dispute.

In mediation parlance, a "panel" is composed of three mediators while a "team" usually denotes two mediators.

For a number of years, especially during World War II, the Federal Mediation and Conciliation Service and its predecessor agency, United States Conciliation Service, made extensive use of the panel approach to the more significant disputes. At one point of time, panels were instituted on a rather rigid, formalistic basis. One of the mediators was designated as chairman, another as associate and the third as secretary. The conference conducted by such panels also followed a formal approach with opening statements by the parties and discussions. In the latter days of World War II, panels became very much less formal and this practice is followed at the present time.

In the mid-50's, the concept of a "team" in lieu of a panel evolved. The adoption of the team approach was dictated in a large measure by limitations of available manpower.

While each technique has merit in specific and selected cases, from a mediation viewpoint, the team concept appears to be the most desirable. Often in a panel situation, the members will caucus by themselves to try to arrive at a meeting of minds on the overall strategy to be employed. Difference of opinions as to the most effective approach inevitably arises. This often leads to an abandonment of a bolder or more affirmative approach in order to achieve an accommodation of the varying panel members' viewpoints. Time is consumed to arrive at a consensus. The members of a team have greater flexibility since an agreement on the techniques to be employed in the particular disputes usually can be arrived at more expeditiously.

Both the panel and team mediation approaches are still utilized in selected cases on a federal level and to a lesser extent on a state level.

Whether mediation intercession takes the form of a panel or team, the basic function is the same--to assist the parties to reach agreement. Such panels or teams exercise no greater or lesser responsibility than a single mediator.

Generally speaking, the cases where panels or teams of mediators are used are those of more than local significance. The intercession of another mediator or mediators is to supplement the efforts of the mediator originally assigned to the dispute.

6 JURISDICTION--FEDERAL, STATE AND LOCAL MEDIATION AGENCIES

In a number of states, both federal and state mediation services are available to the parties. In a few cities and communities, municipal, county or quasi-public mediation facilities have been established. Typical of the latter are New York City's Department of Labor; Toledo's Labor-Management Committee; Nassau County's Mediation Division; and the Louisville Labor-Management Committee.

Where more than one mediation facility is available, parties seeking mediation assistance may be in a quandary as to which mediation agency has jurisdiction in their particular dispute.

There are no tailor-made clearly defined jurisdictional lines between various mediation agencies. Practical as well as legal considerations inhibit any rigidity. The very voluntary nature of the mediation process negates the necessity of strict jurisdictional limitations.

On the federal level, statutory language provides little guidance.

The Labor-Management Relations Act, 1947, as amended, provides in part (Title II, Section 203(b)):

> "The Service may proffer its services in any labor dispute in any industry affecting commerce... whenever in its judgment such dispute threatens to cause a substantial interruption of commerce. The Director and the Service are directed to avoid attempting to mediate disputes which would have only a minor effect on interstate commerce if State or other conciliation services are available to the parties..."

21

There has been no definition or establishment of any specific guidelines by the Federal Mediation and Conciliation Service as to what constitutes a "minor" effect on commerce. Perhaps the experience of the National Labor Relations Board under Section 2(7) of the Labor Management Relations Act, as amended, and the Department of Labor in its administration of the Fair Labor Standards Act in attempting to define even the broader concept of "commerce" under those respective Acts were deterrents from doing so.

The better part of wisdom dictates that the question be more practically handled on an ad hoc basis and the answers conform in a large measure to the availability of a viable state or local mediation agency.

In a memorandum issued in 1950, Director Cyrus Ching stated:

> "The Service believes that a proper interpretation of the Act calls for a statement of jurisdictional policy expressed in general terms, rather than in terms of precise and specific jurisdictional limitations. The service believes that it may accomplish the legislative objective more effectively through a judicious application of the terms of the Act in the light of the general labor-management relations policy of the Government, rather than through a narrow, legal definition of jurisdiction or the establishment of specific formulae."

In the same memorandum, Director Ching outlined the general factors which the Service would utilize in determining whether it should exercise jurisdiction in interstate cases.

a) The volume and dollar value of the product exported from or imported to the State;

b) The nature of the industry or employer establishment and its importance in the industry or economy, local or national, with particular reference to:

22

(1) the degree of integration in the industry and the degree of reliance upon the product or services affected;

(2) the relationship of the dispute to negotiations involving other firms in the industry, other industries, or to the national bargaining policy of the union;

(3) the existence of other sources of supply of the product or service.

c) Number of employees.

An examination of state statutes dealing with the mediation of labor disputes discloses no limitations on their jurisdiction to the extent that each does not even draw a distinction between inter- and intrastate commerce.

In a few states, the statutes set a minimum as to the amount of employees which must be involved before mediation facilities are made available. Illinois and Oklahoma require 25 or more. Montana sets the minimum at 20. Maine and New Hampshire require that there be 10 or more.

Under Section 10A of the Labor-Management Relations Act, the National Labor Relations Board is empowered to cede jurisdiction to state labor relation agencies "even though such cases may involve labor disputes affecting commerce..." No such power of delegation is granted to the Federal Mediation and Conciliation Service.

The only legislative approach to delegation is found in Title II, Section 201(c) which provides:

"The Director may establish suitable procedures for cooperation with State and local mediation agencies."

Soon after the establishment of the Federal Mediation and Conciliation Service as an independent agency, the Service undertook to implement the foregoing provisions of the Act.

The first attempt was characterized by the negotiation of both formal and informal agreements with some of the existing state

23

mediation agencies. As a result of such negotiations, written or oral agreements were consummated with New York, California, Connecticut, Michigan, North Carolina, Pennsylvania and Washington.

The most detailed agreement was with the State of New York. In general, it reserved to the State Board the exclusive right to intercede in intrastate disputes. The State recognized that "it is normally preferable for the Federal Service to handle certain types of disputes of a national or multi-state character which threaten a grave and serious effect on interstate commerce." In the more troublesome area of "minor" versus "major" effect on interstate commerce, the agreement spelled out the primary responsibility of the Federal Service to make the initial determination. However, it further states "it is also recognized that the State agency has an interest in such decisions and that the standards used in making these decisions can be most satisfactorily applied through mutual understanding and consultation between the agencies." The agreement recognized that many disputes would fall into a gray area. In an attempt to set forth guide lines, it was provided that neither agency will attempt to intercede so long as direct negotiations were proceeding satisfactorily and when the services of a mediator were required, the preferences of the parties would be given the greatest weight in determining which agency would mediate.

The efforts of both the State and Federal Mediation services to delineate their respective jurisdictions continued even after these foregoing formal and informal agreements by conferences and consultation between the agencies affected.

Code of Professional Conduct

These efforts culminated in the drafting of the Code of Professional Conduct for Labor Mediators. This Code[5] was finally adopted by the Federal Mediation and Conciliation Service and the several state agencies represented by the Association of Labor Mediation Agencies.

Section 2 of that Code provides in part:

---

5 cf Appendix C

24

"A mediator should not enter any dispute which is
being mediated by another mediator, without first
conferring with the person or persons conducting
such mediation. The mediator should not intercede in a dispute merely because another mediator
may also be participating. Conversely, it should
not be assumed that the lack of mediation participation by one mediator indicates a need for participation by another mediator..."

From an attempt to delineate sharply the jurisdictional bound-
aries of federal and state mediation agencies by formally executed agreements to the Code provisions cited, there has been
a devolution to a mere statement of a modus vivindum.

There are a number of factors which militate against a clear
demarcation of jurisdiction between the federal and state services.

Under the statutory language, even though in a strict sense
any dispute which has more than a minor effect on interstate commerce is within the exclusive responsibility of the federal service, [6] it is not very realistic to expect that a state can divorce
itself from the economic impact of such disputes.

If a plant of a multi-plant, interstate company is the major
industry in a community or state and a stoppage occurs, the municipal or state officials cannot ignore it by asserting that the
matter is being handled by the federal service. Political considerations alone would dictate that they publicly demonstrate their
concern for the community affected. If a mediation service exists
in that state, one of the ways in which these officials can express
their interest is by requesting or instructing their state agency
to intercede and to attempt to bring the dispute to an early termination. Another alternative open is the personal intercession
by the mayor or governor usually by inviting the parties to appear
before them.

The difficulties are multiplied when the dispute fails in the
gray area of major or minor effect on commerce.

---

6 Support for this view is found in General Electric Co. v. Cal-
lahan (294 F2d 60). O.C.A.W. v. Arkansas-Louisiana Gas
Company (332 F2d 64). See also Grand Rapids City Coach Lines
v. Howlett et al (137 F. Supp. 667).

Beyond the political considerations, at least one other factor militates against rigid jurisdictional lines of demarcation.

One or both of the parties may prefer one service or a particular mediator over the other. This is quite understandable since mediation is most successful when the parties have confidence in the mediator's neutrality and ability. Any attempt to interject the other agency in lieu of the one desired by the parties would be either rejected outright or ignored by the parties.

In summary, there is little doubt that Congress has imposed an affirmative responsibility on the Federal Mediation and Conciliation Service to intercede and render mediation assistance in disputes having more than a minor effect on interstate commerce. In the exercise of this exclusive jurisdiction, there must be a recognition that in specific cases, political and practical considerations may dictate joint or concurrent efforts on the part of state public officials or agencies.

Further, it is quite clear that Congress also intended to leave in the exclusive jurisdiction of the state agencies disputes of purely an intrastate character if a viable state mediation agency has been established.

In the gray area of disputes having only a minor effect on interstate commerce, while the initial jurisdictional determination should be made by the federal agency, the best approach appears to be an ad hoc one with the desires or preferences of the parties a weighty consideration in the final determination as to which agency can best assist the parties to resolve their dispute.

Mediation of Grievance Disputes

There have been questions raised as to whether a mediation step could or should be included in a collective bargaining agreement as either the step prior to arbitration or in lieu of arbitration. A number of contracts contain such provisions.

An examination of state mediation acts fails to disclose any expressed statutory prohibition on state mediators serving grievance disputes.

As far as the federal service is concerned, prior to the passage of the Labor-Management Relations Act there were no limitations on the assumption of jurisdiction over grievance disputes.

26

Since arbitration as the terminal point of the grievance procedure had not attained its present-day acceptability, mediation was often found to be an acceptable alternative. In other contracts, provision was made for the intercession of a mediator prior to the submission of the dispute to arbitration.

However, with the passage of the Labor-Management Relations Act limitations were placed on the federal service.

. Section 203(c) of that Act provides:

> "Final adjustment by a method agreed upon by the parties is hereby declared to be the desirable method for the settlement of grievance disputes arising over the application or interpretation of an existing collective bargaining agreement. The Service is directed to make its conciliation and mediation service available in the settlement of such grievance disputes only as a last resort and in exceptional cases."

Apart from the grumblings of one senator, that the foregoing provisions tended to shackle the Director in his mediation efforts, the legislative history of the Act fails to shed light on the reasons for the limitations.

The Director of the newly established Federal Mediation and Conciliation Service was faced with the problem of translating the legislative direction into workable internal policy.

One of the dilemmas was the apparent contradiction in the statutory language. Section 203(c) states that the method agreed upon by the parties for the disposition of grievances is the desirable method. Assuming that the parties during the course of their negotiations decided that mediation should be utilized either as a step before or in lieu of arbitration, could the Service refuse to honor it? Further, did the second sentence, which clearly prohibits the Director from interceding in grievance disputes unless it was an exceptional case or a last resort, grant him authority to withhold mediation services despite the parties' contractual agreement?

Another problem was whether existing contracts which provided for mediation should be honored, and what would be the Service policy with respect to future contracts.

Lastly, the terms "exceptional" and "last resort" had to be defined.

Motivated in a large measure by limitations of budget and manpower, the Federal Service adopted policies and procedures designed to carry forward the Congressional mandate.[7]

In essence, these policies and procedures provide that when a request is received for mediation assistance in a grievance dispute, a determination is first made by the Regional Director as to whether the dispute falls into the category of an exceptional or last resort case. If it does not, the Service assigns a mediator to the case for certain limited purposes. The mediator so assigned will normally urge the parties to utilize the grievance or arbitration procedures of their collective bargaining contract. If their contract does not provide adequate procedures, he will assist the parties in structuring a procedure for the purpose of settling the immediate issue in dispute. He will endeavor to avoid discussion of the merits of the grievance and concentrate instead on a method of adjustment.

If the grievance falls into the category of exceptional or last resort, the mediator will be instructed to address himself to the merits of the particular grievance and assist the parties to resolve it.

Further, mediators were instructed to discourage parties from inserting into their contracts provisions for mediation as part of the grievance procedure.

---

7 See Appendix D

7 CONTRIBUTIONS A MEDIATOR MAY MAKE TO THE NEGOTIATIONS

When various writers seek to describe the role of a mediator in a labor dispute, they generally resort to generalities such as "He is a catalytic agent," or "He serves as a conduit for channeling information."

The difficulty with such broad statements is that they have a negative connotation.

If the parties properly utilize the services of a mediator, he can make an affirmative contribution to the resolution of the labor dispute.

There are a number of specific areas in which this may be accomplished.

1. Utilizing the Mediator's Training and Experience.

All applicants for the Federal Mediation and Conciliation Service must have had seven years of full-time progressively responsible and successful experience in collective bargaining or in other closely allied fields of labor-management relations before they are seriously considered. After appointment, the mediator's skills are constantly updated by workshops and self-improvement devices.

The average federal mediator handles 36 cases a year and actively participates in over 124 joint collective bargaining meetings. The experience he acquires in conducting collective bargaining conferences far exceeds the experience acquired by most representatives of management or labor. This experience provides him with a reservoir of knowledge not only as to the techniques of bargaining but also, and equally important, the knowledge of how other parties have resolved specific issues. This experience will equip him to formulate alternatives which may enable the parties to accommodate their conflicting viewpoints.

29

2. A Mediator Can Advise and Counsel As To The Timing of Offers and Counterproposals.

Often the key to an agreement is the timing of an offer or counterproposal. Because of the mediator's neutrality, he is in the best position to assess the receptivity for a proposal or counterproposal. All too often, an offer or counterproposal which would otherwise be acceptable is rejected out of hand because it was made prematurely. If made too late, the climate of agreement has past and the offer is no longer palatable.

The mediator can judge better than a partisan when his counterpart is conditioned to accept the less perfect solution and when the offer or counterproposal may be timely.

3. The Training and Experience of a Mediator Has Equipped Him to be a Master of the Alternative.

All too often, parties can only visualize the problem in their own frame of reference. They become so engrossed in their own positions that they fail to see the different approaches to the solution of the problem which is creating the impasse. An experienced mediator has encountered many similar situations and knows how other negotiators have solved the same problem without the necessity of total capitulation. As a result, he can suggest these alternative solutions to the parties and guide the discussions at the bargaining table so that the pathway to solution becomes viable to each party.

An illustrative situation occurred not many years ago. A mediator was called into a dispute involving a protracted strike. The union had continued negotiations for one month beyond the expiration date of the contract before striking. After a number of joint and separate meetings, he was able to assist the parties in resolving all of the issues except retroactivity. The company insisted that it never granted retroactivity in any of its prior negotiations and would not depart from that principle. The union was equally adamant and insisted that no settlement was possible unless it provided for retroactivity. By careful probing, the mediator became aware that the company feared that many of its highly skilled employees had obtained other employment during the strike and that there existed some doubt as to whether such employees would return to work at the conclusion of the strike. Based on his experience in prior cases, the mediator suggested that an amount closely approximating the lump sum which would have been due each employee if retroactivity had been granted be set aside as a financial inducement for employees to return to work. He further suggested that this sum be paid to employees who returned to work within three days of the settlement and remained on the job for 30 days after such return. This suggested alternative approach provided the basis for a resolution of the dispute.

4. A Mediator Can Avoid Emotional Crisis.

It is axiomatic in collective bargaining that whenever emotions supplant reasoning, agreement is impossible. All too often when emotions are high, parties in the heat of the argument may take an end position prematurely. Having done so, it may be difficult for them to retreat from it when a later accommodation is advanced.

A mediator is ever alert to this danger and can avoid an emotional crisis by the judicious use of the caucus device or by asserting his chairmanship and directing the discussions to a less emotional issue.

5. A Mediator Can Assist the Parties to Explore Avenues of Accommodation.

Perhaps one of the major functions performed by the mediator relates to exploration of offers. Often one party may want to gauge the receptivity of an approach to a problem without formalizing it into an offer and thus destroy or jeopardize a bargaining posture. If the mediator is apprised of this desire, he can put forth the approach to the other party as the mediator's suggestion. If the suggestion is acceptable then the first party can formalize it into an offer. If it is not acceptable, the first party's bargaining position is preserved.

6. A Mediator May Initiate a Desired Meeting.

Often when meetings have been recessed and especially where they have been adjourned subject to call, one of the parties may desire a meeting but fear that if they request the meeting it may be construed prematurely as a change in their bargaining position or as a signal of capitulation.

If the mediator is advised of the problem, he may initiate the call of the meeting based on his appraisal of the necessity and thus take the onus of its call upon his shoulders. The party who desired the meeting then can reluctantly accept without running the risk of endangering at the outset their bargaining posture.

7. A Mediator Can Assist the Parties in Formulation and Structuring Their Offers or Counterproposals.

There are well-accepted devices for assuring the maximum saleability of an offer.

A mediator can assist the parties to formulate their offers or counterproposals in such a way as to assure that they will have a high degree of receptivity. Many times it is as simple as couching the offer in affirmative terms and avoiding a negative introduction.

As an illustration, one of the issues in a dispute may involve the question of shop stewards leaving their workbench to process a grievance and the necessity of obtaining the foreman's permission to do so.

Expressing the offer as "no steward shall leave his work area without the permission of his foreman" is almost certain to create resentment and quick rejection.

If the same offer was stated in the affirmative such as "stewards shall have the right to leave their work areas with the permission" a different reaction could be expected.

In the final hours of most negotiations the issues remaining in dispute become narrowed to four or five. At this point, most practitioners start the process of packaging offers and counterproposals.

In such "packages", the thrust is to treat it as a totality and not permit the other party to pick and choose among the various items which comprise the package. Illustrative of this technique of bargaining would be an offer whereby one party suggests that if the other party would withdraw its demands on issues 1, 3, and 5, it would be willing to accede to demands 2 and 4. Theoretically, the demanding party cannot counter by saying it accepts the concession on 2 and 4 and in addition wants demands 1 and 5. The concession on 2 and 4 was made contingent on withdrawal of 1, 3, and 5, and would not have been made unless withdrawal was acceptable.

The timing and structuring of such packages are often crucial. Here, too, the mediator can make a positive contribution to the final settlement.

Such packages are often rejected because of the order in which issues are presented.

A negative reaction can well be anticipated if in the presentation of the package mention is made at the very outset of the items which must be withdrawn before mention is made of the items on which there are concessions.

A much more desirable method would be to outline first the concessions and then the withdrawals on which they are predicated. Even in presenting the concessions, the better practice is to choose as the lead-off item the concession on the issue in which the other party has indicated the greatest interest.

8. A Mediator Is Alert to the Interplay of Intra-Company and Union Politics.

Since labor organizations are economic institutions operating in a political environment, the crosscurrents of political aspirations may well dictate the union's posture at the bargaining table.

Similarly, internal company politics often lead the negotiator to be overcautious in his approaches. He becomes quite sensitive to the possibility of second-guessing with its job security threat. Under such circumstances, the company negotiator will seek to spread the decision making responsibility to avoid subsequent criticism. The bargaining table flexibility so essential to agreement is thereby impaired.

These factors cannot be ignored at the bargaining table since their presence will impede settlement.

A mediator is alert to these overtones and very often can take on the burden of urging or advocating solutions to the issues so that each party can avoid the necessity of being the initiator.

33

In the proper case, the mediator can incorporate his suggestions in a formal or informal recommendation to the parties with the possibility of making such recommendations public. Here, too, the parties are relieved of the responsibility of identification with the accommodations necessary for agreement.

At times this may not involve the substantive issues but questions of procedure.

Illustratively, a problem may arise with the union negotiating committee as to conveying back an offer with a committee recommendation to the membership. While the individual members of the committee may be persuaded that it is a fair and equitable offer, the politics of the situation may dictate that they do not become too closely associated with it. In such situations, the mediator can suggest that the offer be submitted to the membership and that the vote be taken by secret ballot. In support of his suggestion, he can direct the parties' attention to Section 203(c) of the Labor-Management Relations Act[8] which authorizes him to make such suggestions.

9. <u>A Mediator Can Assist the Parties to Minimize the Possibility of Rejection of a Tentative Agreement.</u>

One of the problems in recent years has been the relatively high rate of rejections by union negotiating committees of tentative agreements reached at the bargaining table.

This interjects an instability into the collective bargaining relationships which can be destructive of the whole process.

There are a number of techniques which a mediator can suggest which will minimize the possibility of a rejection. These will be more fully described in the chapter on minimizing rejections.

---

[8]   See Appendix B

8 CONFIDENTIALITY

As previously mentioned the policy of the United States is to rely on collective bargaining and mediation as the principal means of resolving industrial conflicts. To effectuate that policy mediators must not only be impartial but must be considered so by both parties to a labor dispute. In addition, the parties must be free to talk without risking subsequent disclosure of their confidence. Such confidence and disclosures are wholly voluntary and cannot be compelled by a mediator, but without them mediation would cease to be effective in settling labor disputes.

Some examples of the kinds of disclosures made to mediators are personal idiosyncrasies of representatives of labor and management, financial condition of the company or union, competitive problems, internal frictions, facts contained in the confidential records and files of both parties and end positions which may be premature if advanced at the bargaining table at the time the disclosure is made.

The rules of the Federal Mediation and Conciliation Service relating to confidentiality are contained in Title 29, Chapter XII Code of Federal Regulations which reflects the regulations adopted by that Service.[9] These regulations in effect prohibit any disclosure by any employee of the Service of information, oral or written, received by them in the course of their official activities without prior approval of the Director of the Service.

Several of the states, either by statute or regulations have similar provisions. Notable among these are Connecticut, Maine, Michigan, New Hampshire, New York, and North Carolina.

There are some significant differences in these statutes. In the Federal Mediation and Conciliation Service regulations the

[9] See Appendix F

only person who can waive the privilege is the Director of the Service. The waiver of the privilege by either or both parties is not determinative of the question whether the privilege should be waived. The theory of the Service is predicated on public policy.

In Connecticut, the privilege of non-disclosure can be waived by the party who supplied the information.[10]

The New Hampshire statute[11] provides:

> "Neither the proceedings or any part thereof, before the labor commissioner by virtue of the foregoing provisions of this subdivision shall be received in evidence for any purpose in any judicial proceeding before any other court or tribunal."

Under the foregoing provision, there is a question whether a disclosure can be compelled before a nonjudicial tribunal such as a legislative committee.

The New York, Florida, and North Carolina statutes[12] specifically foreclose the possibility of a forced disclosure before an administrative as well as a judicial body.

The one exception to the rule of confidentiality made in several states is where the subject of inquiry involves the commission of a crime.

Both the courts and administrative tribunals have respected the rule of confidentiality when it was brought into question.

The inherent power of the executive branch of the government to refuse to disclose evidence contrary to the best interest of the Government has been recognized since Marbury v. Madison (1 Cranch 37). The non-disclosure regulations of the Federal Mediation and Conciliation Service has been upheld by the National Labor Relations Board in International Furniture (106 NLRB 127) and in Tomlinson of High Point (75 NLRB 681, 685).

---

[10] Connecticut General Statutes Annotated, Title 31, Section 100.
[11] Chapter 210, Section 18
[12] New York Labor Laws Article 21, Chapter 31, Sec. 754(3).
North Carolina, Chapter 95, Article 1, Sec. 36.
Florida, Chapter 57-306 of Laws of 1957.

In the latter case, the Board stated:

"However useful the testimony of a conciliator might be... to execute successfully their function of assisting in the settlement of labor disputes, the conciliators must maintain a reputation for impartiality, and the parties to the conciliation conferences must feel free to talk without any fear that the conciliator may subsequently make disclosures as a witness in some other proceeding, to the disadvantage of a party to the conference.... The inevitable result would be that the usefulness of the Conciliation Service in the settlement of future disputes would be seriously impaired, if not destroyed. The resultant injury to the public interest would clearly outweigh the benefit to be derived from making their testimony available in particular cases." (See also New Britain Machine Company--105 NLRB 646)

Acceptability of a mediator and his effectiveness in a given dispute is directly related to the confidence both parties have in his professional abilities and his maintenance of confidence disclosed to him in the performance of his official duties. If mediation is to be effective, the privilege of non-disclosure should be an absolute one. It should be the privilege of a public officer (such as the mediator) and not the privilege of the parties to the dispute.

9 OBTAINING THE SERVICES OF A FEDERAL MEDIATOR

The Labor-Management Relations Act provides in part in Section 203(b):

> "The Service may proffer its services in any labor dispute in any industry affecting commerce, either upon its own motion or upon request of one or more of the parties to a dispute...."

Section 8(d) of the same Act provides in part:

> "That where there is in effect a collective bargaining contract covering employees in an industry affecting commerce, the duty to bargain collectively shall also mean that no party to such contract shall terminate or modify such contract unless the party desiring such termination and modification--
> (1) serves a written notice upon the other party ...of the proposed termination or modification sixty days prior to the expiration date...
> (2) notifies the Federal Mediation and Conciliation Service within 30 days after such notice of the existence of a dispute and simultaneously therewith notifies any State or Territorial agency established to mediate and conciliate disputes within the state or territory where the dispute occurred, provided no agreement has been reached by that time...."

These statutory provisions spell out the ways which authorize a federal mediator to intercede in a dispute.

The first method is "upon its own motion." Normally this method of intercession is confined to disputes arising over the negotiations of a new contract. In such cases no 30-day notice is required by Section 8(d)3 quoted above since that section relates to disputes over the termination or modification of an existing collective bargaining contract.

In rare cases, the Federal Mediation and Conciliation Service will enter a dispute on its own motion at the request of some federal, state or local governmental agency if notified by such agencies that the dispute is having an impact on either the defense effort or the economic well-being of the community.

The more common method for the intercession of the federal mediator is as a result of compliance by the parties with Section 8(d)3. The federal service has prepared for the convenience of the parties a 30-day notice form (F-7).[13]

While there is no statutory requirement that this particular form be used, the information elicited by the form assures an orderly processing of the case by the agency.

The failure to file the statutory notice to the Federal Mediation and Conciliatory Service and, where appropriate, to State and Territorial Agency, may expose the party seeking modification or termination to legal penalties. It has been held[14] that if the union fails to file the required notice a strike called to compel modification or termination of a contract is illegal and the employees engaging in the stoppage lose their status as "employees" protected by the Labor-Management Relations Act.[15] A similar ruling was applied to an employer who invoked a lockout without notifying the Federal Mediation and Conciliation Service and terminated the contract.[16] If the notice to the conciliation agencies is late, the union must wait until 30 days have expired after the actual filing of the notice before calling a strike.[17]

---

13 See Appendix G
14 See Appendix H
15 Retail Clerks--J.C. Penney, 109 NLRB 754. IAM-International Continental Engine, 177 NLRB #60.
16 Bakers Council of Greater New York, 174 NLRB.
17 Retail Clerks vs. NLRB, 265 F2d 814.

The 30-day notice should be filed with the regional office of the Federal Mediation Service which has jurisdiction over the situs of the plant affected by the dispute. On the reverse side of Form F-7 is a listing of the addresses of the various regional offices and the geographical area over which they have jurisdiction.

The third method which will evoke the intercession of a federal mediator is a request by either management or labor. It need not be a joint request nor need it be in writing. An oral request is sufficient.

On receipt of a 30-day notice or a request, the regional office will screen out those cases which are obviously purely intrastate. All other cases are assigned to a Commissioner stationed at or near the site of the dispute. The Commissioner has the duty to contact the parties to the dispute to ascertain facts which can assist the Regional Director to determine whether the dispute is one which meets the Service's jurisdictional requirements and the possible need for mediational assistance. If he reaches an affirmative conclusion on both considerations, the dispute is assigned to a Commissioner for mediation. Normally the Commissioner who conducted the original investigation is given the assignment.

At this point, it is the responsibility of the assigned mediator to keep himself fully advised of the progress of the negotiations and intercede if the need for mediation assistance arises.

If there is a need for mediation assistance, if the mediator follows traditional practice, he will confer first with the party who has either requested assistance or who filed the 30-day notice. During this conference, he will seek to obtain a grasp of the issues causing the dispute and that party's viewpoint. He then will confer with the other party to ascertain his position on the issues involved.

After he has completed these separate conferences and has reached the conclusion that mediation assistance is needed, the mediator will schedule a joint conference of the parties.

The conference will normally be held on neutral territory. If a Federal Mediation Office is readily accessible, that will be the place of the meeting. If such facilities are not available, he will schedule the meeting at any convenient location as other federal facilities, hotel or motel.

If non-federal facilities are utilized, the rental expenses are borne by the Service. If the parties desire to meet at some other location, mutually acceptable, the parties will normally divide the expenses between themselves.

10 CONDUCTING JOINT MEETINGS

After a meeting place has been agreed to by both parties, the mediator is then confronted with the problem of conducting the joint conference in such a manner as will ease tensions, create an atmosphere which will lead to fruitful discussion and enable him to make the most effective mediation contribution to the dispute.

Introduction and Appearances

While the mediator may be acquainted with the principal spokesmen for each party, he is seldom familiar with the individual committee members.

The management team may be composed of three or more people in addition to the spokesman. They are selected by the company because of their familiarity with production problems or with the various grievance disputes which have arisen during the contract term.

The union negotiating committee generally is composed of the business agent or international representative, some if not all of the local union officers and committeemen. The latter are usually elected from among the shop employees and these individuals may vary from contract year to contract year.

The mediator should introduce himself to all present and not merely to the principal spokesmen for each side. To many of those serving on negotiating teams there is a matter of pride-- especially on the union's side. Often, many are undergoing their first experience as negotiators. They have been singled out by their fellow workers to represent them and justly feel a sense of urgent responsibility. They are at once proud of their status and suspicious of an "outsider." All too often they are not quite certain in their own minds as to the exact functions of a mediator. A warm and informal introduction may do much to abate some of the suspicions and fears.

After the introduction, the appearances of those present should be recorded. This can be done rather informally. Many experienced mediators use the device of passing out two sheets of paper--one to each side--each containing two columns. One column is headed "Name", the other column "Position and Title". Both sides are requested to fill in the called for information and return it to the mediator.

Upon receipt of the list, a good mediator will endeavor to familiarize himself with the listed names and to identify the individuals present with the names without appearing to do so.

He will particularly try to fix first names in his mind. While he should avoid addressing people by their first names at a joint conference--it is invaluable to use first names when talking to each side during a caucus. Use of first names during separate conferences often breaks through the barrier of formality and establishes a camaraderie which leads to freer and franker discussion of the issues.

The use of first names has of course its limitations. There are some people who resent being addressed by their first name. This is particularly true on management's side. Whether they are motivated by a feeling of superiority, or the need of maintaining dignity or status in the eyes of their subordinates is of little importance. The good mediator should be quick to sense this feeling and respect it if he is to succeed in assisting the parties to arrive at an agreement.

Control of the Meeting

A mediator is neither the agent nor the broker of management or labor. He represents in a large measure the public interest and is carrying out a statutory responsibility.

A mediation meeting is his meeting and not that of the parties. The final determination should lie with him as to when a recess, caucus or adjournment is to be called.

To achieve this control over the meeting, it is necessary for him to establish the fact of his chairmanship at the very outset of the meeting. He can do so physically by occupying the chair at the head of the conference table between both parties.

A good mediator should never permit himself to be relegated to the role of an observer. By the same token, the mediator should not become the autocrat of the conference table. He can readily accede to the desires of the parties for recesses and adjournments, but in doing so should make it clear that requests should be addressed to him and that he consents to them.

Since it is his meeting, he should insist that the parties carry on their discussions in a dignified manner. There should at the same time be a realization that negotiating meetings are not prayer meetings--that the language indulged in is many times more forceful and picturesque than that used in family living rooms. Many times bargaining postures dictate role playing by the representatives of the parties. Real or assumed indignation, shock, surprise, impatience, threats of economic reprisals, humor--in fact, a display of the whole range of human emotions--are all part and parcel of the collective bargaining process.

The repeated use of bucolic or profane language should be discouraged as much as possible. To permit it to run rampant seriously impairs the effectiveness of the mediator and the success of the negotiations. Despite the facade of being "tough" or thick-skinned, most people are normally offended when exposed to profane diatribes. They impress no thinking person and lower the dignity of the entire meeting.

Similarly, it is inimical to agreement-making to permit parties to indulge in personal abuse or attack. The objective of a negotiating session is to attempt to compose the differences between the parties so that agreement can be achieved. Personality clashes have no place at the bargaining table. At the best, they are roadblocks to agreement. A personal attack almost always gives rise to a reply in kind. Tempers are substituted for reason. Areas of disagreement are widened and often positions are taken in the heat of argument from which graceful retreat becomes impossible.

In the heat of negotiations, several parties very often try to speak at the same time. The conference then becomes a series of conferences without a common objective. Such "cross fire" can quickly destroy any progress being made in the negotiations. "Cross fire" is normally born of a desire to "get into the act" or of a committee member's feelings of frustration when he feels he is being ignored. Nothing can be achieved unless the chairman quickly discourages the cross fire and insists that the meeting proceed through one spokesman at a time. Most spokesmen will readily assist the mediator to bring cross fire under control since it also impinges on their prerogatives. Beyond causing the meeting to deteriorate to a vocal brawl, cross fire often reveals weaknesses in bargaining positions which may jeopardize the successful achievement of one or the other party's objectives.

Right to Attend Meeting

In multi-plant operations, because of the chronology of organization, separate certifications may exist for the individual plants and result in separate contracts. Generally speaking, most companies prefer to negotiate each contract separately. Again generally, labor organizations prefer to negotiate on a company-wide basis leading to a master agreement. When the companies resist the demand for company-wide bargaining, unions may resort to having representatives of the other plants either as members of the negotiating committee or as "observers." In this way, unions feel that they can assure uniformity and condition the company representatives to accept the concept of company-wide bargaining in the future.

The insistence of the union to have representatives of the other plants at the bargaining table often presents nice problems for the mediator. When the company observes the presence of these "outsiders," it reacts rather violently such as threatening to walk out of the meeting or refusing to go forward with negotiations unless the "outsiders" are excluded from the meeting room.

The Labor-Management Relations Act, 1947, provides:

"Employees shall have the right to self organization, to form, join or assist labor organizations, to bargain collectively through representatives of their own choosing...."

45

It is therefore quite clear that the employees have a statutory right to select anyone they desire to act as their representative or spokesman. There is also a correlative right of management to select whomsoever it chooses to act as its representative. While this is not an absolute right, the Board and the Courts are reluctant to deny it except in very extreme cases.

Consequently, if the "outsiders" have been designated as part of the negotiating committee of the particular plant involved, they have a legal right to attend and participate in the negotiating session. If the company refuses to meet under these circumstances, it may be risking an unfair labor practice charge.

The difficulty lies in circumstances in which the "outsiders" are attending as observers. The constitution of the American Newspaper Guild expressly provides that all union members in the bargaining unit have a right to attend bargaining conferences as observers. If the number of members in the unit is 150, the two or three management representatives may be faced with a rather formidable array across the table.

An adherence by both parties to their position blocks discussion necessary to resolution of the dispute. The mediator must find some accommodation of viewpoints which will permit the meeting to go forward. Failing to persuade the "observer" to withdraw or the company to continue, he may use one of many approaches. He may persuade the "observers" to withdraw from the conference room and to occupy another room on the premises. In this manner, they are readily accessible to the union negotiating committee for consultation, advice and guidance. He may be able to persuade the company to go forward with the meeting on the union's agreement that the "observers" will respect certain ground rules such as limiting their activities to merely observing and not participating in the discussions across the table.

Another approach that may be used is to carry forward with the meeting by having the parties in separate meeting rooms with no joint meetings and the mediator to shuttle back and forth between them. Normally, this is an awkward and unproductive method of operation but in the situation outlined above may be the only device open to the mediator to get by the roadblock.

Statement of Issues

After the introduction and appearance taking, the mediator is prepared to go forward with the conference.

Generally, the first order of business is a statement of issues still remaining unsolved. Emphasis should be placed on a discussion of only the unresolved issues. It must be borne in mind that before the advent of mediation, the parties undoubtedly must have been meeting by themselves and, in most cases, have reached tentative agreement on a number of issues.

Experience teaches that to ask the parties to review issues already tentatively resolved hampers progress in negotiations and may open up a Pandora's box.

Normally, the party making the demands is requested to start the recitation of the unresolved issues. Since generally it is the union which is seeking to modify the existing collective bargaining agreement, it is the proper party to make the first presentation.

The mediator should permit the union spokesman to present the issues in his own way. He should not attempt to advise the union representative what issues he should address himself to first.

While the presentation of the demands should not be in too great a depth, it should be sufficient enough to give the mediator a good grasp of the scope and complexity of the problems he is facing. Often a mediator is confronted with a presentation so sketchy that it is impossible for him to intelligently appraise the dispute. Some business agents will state: "We have five demands --union security, vacations, holidays, wage and seniority," and then sit back expecting the mediator by some Divine revelation to know exactly what the problem may be.

If such a presentation is made, the mediator should draw out a fuller picture by adroit questioning such as:

What form of union security is requested?

What form of union security did the expired or expiring contract provide?

What modifications or additions in the holiday and vacation program are being sought?

47

What were the provisions of the old contract?

Seniority, for example, is a multifaceted problem. Inquiry must be made to ascertain the general areas of seniority which the union is seeking to modify.

The questioning at this stage must be so worded as not to place the union representative in a position of justifying or defending its demands. The purpose of the questioning at the first joint meeting is to elicit information and not to persuade or change any party's position.

After the union has presented its demands, the company is then called upon to respond and to present such counterproposals as it may desire. Not too many years ago management confined its remarks to a rebuttal of the union's requests. However, the collective bargaining picture has changed. Management is now interposing meaningful demands and has a right to present them at the bargaining table. Many of these demands are attempts by management to recapture so-called management prerogatives lost in prior bargaining or through loose management practices at plant levels.

Art of Listening

One of the principal keys to successful mediation efforts used by the mediator is the art of listening.

The development and application of this art enables a mediator to sense the areas of possible agreement, not only during the first statement of the issues, but also during the course of future joint and separate conferences.

The emphasis or lack of emphasis placed by the parties on particular issues, the use of negotiating language, "smoke signals" indulged in--all when properly evaluated may point out approaches to the final resolution of the dispute.

Not many years ago, a large West Coast manufacturer was the target of the first strike called by its union in its entire industrial history. The reason for the strike was evident. A rival union had successfully negotiated a settlement at a competitive company. The same rival union was raiding the other union. To stave off further inroads on its membership, the union had to be able to produce a settlement which exceeded that obtained by the raiding union.

The manufacturer, not only for competitive reasons, but also as a member of an industry association, was committed not to exceed the pattern established by the competing company. When the company refused to exceed the pattern, the union for its own survival had to resort to strike. Mediation was requested.

At the first meeting, in its rebuttal to the union's request for improvements in the health and welfare provisions of the old contract, the company stated that it could find no basis for the demand since it prided itself in being the leader of the industry in this specific field. This remark was the key to the solution of a costly strike. The mediator, exercising his art of listening, made a mental note of the company's statement. During the course of the subsequent discussions, he was able to develop that the competitor had so improved his health and welfare contract provisions that it equalled that of the struck employee. As a result, it was no longer the leader. When the parties were conditioned for a mediator's suggestion, he persuaded the company to revise its health and welfare offer so that it would retain its leadership status. In terms of cost--not benefits--the improvements amounted to a fraction of a cent. In terms of benefits, the union could properly go before its membership and present a better package to them than that obtained by the raiding union. A strike was settled because the mediator exercised the art of listening.

Evaluation of Issues

During the course of the presentation of the issues, a mediator should make an evaluation of the issues. Such an evaluation can not only provide him with a better perspective of the dispute, but often enables him to know where the emphasis of his mediation efforts should be placed as negotiations progress.

Issues can be first segregated into economic and non-economic. These are some items which have a direct cost impact such as wages, holidays, vacations, shift premiums and the like. There are other items which are clearly non-cost items such as union security, some aspects of seniority, and grievance procedure. Other items fall into a gray area--work rules and seniority areas are examples which have an indirect cost impact and may be difficult to classify.

Issues can be further separated into strike and non-strike issues. Wages and issues affecting job security are normally strike issues. Union security, unless coupled with a job security or wage issue, is not an issue which normally will support a prolonged stoppage. Disputes relating to grievance procedure, superseniority, leaves of absence and the like are not normally issues upon which a union would engage in a strike.

Coupling of Issues

During the presentation of the outstanding issues, and often aided by the evaluations suggested above, the mediator can mentally couple interdependent or related issues and thus plan his approach to the solution of some of the issues.

To illustrate coupling of issues--a union may be seeking to strengthen the union security provisions of an expiring contract. It may also be demanding automatic progressions in the rate ranges to the maximum where the contract provided for automatic progressions only to the midpoint with merits thereafter. The reason behind the union request for automatic progression to the maximum may be its fear that a merit band in a rate range is or could be used to discriminate against employees active in the union. A strengthening of the union security provisions would dispel this fear and remove the necessity for management to make concessions in the rate range provisions.

As negotiations progress, the exercise of the art of successfully coupling can materially narrow the issues and lead to a logical packaging of the last remaining issues.

Stipulation of Total Agreement

Often during the course of a conference, a mediator discovers that one party or the other appears reluctant to modify its position on a particular issue or to withdraw a proposal or counterproposal because of the fear that in doing so its position on that issue would be irretrievably gone.

If this situation is permitted to continue, little, if any, progress can be made in the negotiations. This is particularly true if there is a multiplicity of issues. To achieve settlement, issues must be discussed, explored, and disposed of, either by agreement or withdrawal. To pass them and leave them in limbo can, at the very least, unduly prolong the dispute.

Under such circumstances, mediators often have utilized the stipulation of a total agreement. In essence, the parties in the joint meeting are requested to stipulate that "any concession, modification or withdrawal of any particular issue made by any of the parties is for the purpose of arriving at a full agreement --if no agreement is reached either or both parties are free to revert to any position they deem advisable on all the issues."

Experience indicates that this is usually readily adopted by the parties. It protects their respective bargaining postures and at the same time permits the tentative disposition of issues so that the negotiations can go forward.

11 CAUCUSES

✳ When Caucus Should Be Called

In the mediation process, the most effective reconciliation of differences occurs during the separate meetings or caucuses of the parties with the mediator. In a caucus, the mediator need not be as sensitive to the preservation of a bargaining position as in a joint conference. The parties are freer to talk in separate conference where their adversaries are not present.

When the joint conference should be abandoned temporarily in favor of continuing bargaining through caucuses or separate conferences does at times pose problems. A number of general rules can be evolved as to when a request for a caucus should be made.

1. When the discussions at the joint conference become so heated that emotions are supplanting reason and a continuation may cause participants to take extreme positions from which retreat would be difficult, a caucus called at this point can provide a needed cooling off period.

2. When the joint discussions have reached a stage where no further progress is being made and the parties are becoming merely repetitive.

3. Where one of the parties in the joint discussions has indicated a possible area of compromise. A caucus at this point will give the mediator an opportunity to develop an area of agreement. In such an event, the first caucus should be held with the party who indicated the possible area of compromise.

4. If neither side has indicated any flexibility in their bargaining position, the first caucus should be held with the party appearing most inflexible. In such situations, some movement is necessary if negotiations are to proceed along fruitful lines. Under these circumstances, the mediator, by probing during the caucus, should attempt to review with the intransigent party the consequences of its continued adherence to its position--no agreement--possible economic dislocation.

5. The mediator should be alert to forestall one party from taking an end position prematurely. Many times in the heat of joint discussions, one party or the other may take a final position on an issue. Having taken such a position in the presence of the other side, pride dictates that that position be adhered to regardless of the change in bargaining climate. Compromise or withdrawal becomes difficult. Often, too, an expressed rigidity on one issue prematurely will prevent any progress on other pending issues. Effective mediation requires fluidity. An alert mediator who can anticipate that one party is about to take an end position prematurely at the joint bargaining session can do much to further advance bargaining by requesting a caucus.

end here.

Political Problems in Caucuses

At times, it may appear advantageous to have a separate meeting with only the principal without his committee.

Before such a meeting is attempted, the mediator must first ascertain if such principal is at liberty to do so. There are some union negotiating committees who object to their spokesman conferring alone with the other side or even with a mediator. Even though this attitude is both shortsighted and nonsensical, it is nevertheless a reality which must be faced. In such instances, the mediator would create unnecessary barriers to an agreement if he insists upon meeting with the principal alone. The principal would be placed in a politically dangerous position if he accepts and an embarrassing one if he refuses to so meet.

53

While the problem is normally encountered with union committees, it also occurs, though with less frequency, with management groups, expecially if there is an outside attorney or consultant with whom the mediator desires to meet alone. The "resident" labor relations man is apt to feel that he is being bypassed and may refuse to accede to a compromise, not because of its merits but because he wants to demonstrate his importance in the scheme of things.

12 DEVELOPING HABITS OF AGREEMENT

In many cases, the mediator is confronted with a large number of unresolved issues. The problem then arises as to what specific issues or groups of issues should be discussed first.

A guiding principle is to discuss first those issues which appear the most susceptible of solution. The purpose of this approach is to establish a habit of agreement. If agreement can be achieved on some of the easier issues, hostility is dispelled and the parties made to realize that there are some common grounds between them. The momentum of the agreement on some of these issues may carry over to the more difficult unresolved issues.

If no issue or issues appear easier of solution, then generally it is wise to leave the economic issues to the last. The purchasing power of an additional cent or fraction of a cent cannot be under-rated. Often bitterly urged noneconomic demands dissipate with an additional monetary offer. If the situation is reversed, the parties may find themselves in a position of having reached a tentative understanding on money matters and still far from agreement because of an emotionally charged noneconomic issue.

Exploration of Positions in Depth

As pointed out before, the separate conference or caucus gives the mediator greater latitude in exploring issues than a joint conference.

A mediator should utilize the separate conference to explore the issues in depth. Very often demands are generalities. They represent an attempt to formulate in general terms a number of related or unrelated grievances which have arisen during the contract term.

55

By exploring the reasons which gave rise to a demand, a mediator often finds that the real area of disagreement is much narrower than the general demand indicates. This is particularly true with respect to demands involving seniority, shift assignment, and distribution of overtime. Often these are based on specific grievances--usually involving a breakdown of communications. By addressing the discussion to the specific grievances rather than to the formalized demand, agreement becomes possible.

Exploration vs. Offers

Very often during the course of a separate conference, based on the suggestions of either the mediator or the party, a possible area of agreement is developed which should be conveyed to the other party.

The manner in which such possibility is conveyed to the other party then becomes important. Many times the party who accepts the suggestion or initiates it may desire to preserve his bargaining position if the possibility is unattractive to the other party. In such cases, the mediator must be quite circumspect as to the manner in which he discusses the problem with the other party. If he unwittingly conveys it as an offer, he destroys the bargaining position of the party. He should and must convey it either as his suggestion or as an approach which might be fruitful if in the judgment of his listener it has possibilities of leading to a solution.

If the party with whom he first confers decides to make it a formal offer, the mediator should so convey it, either alone at a separate conference with the other party or else suggest it to be communicated directly at a joint conference.

Sometimes an allegedly sharp negotiator will attempt to get the mediator to convey to the other party as the mediator's suggestion a completely irresponsible offer or approach. The mediator is under no obligation to do so. Throughout the negotiations, the mediator must so conduct himself as to evoke the respect and confidence of both parties. If he were to lend himself to any such maneuver, he would destroy his effectiveness. Under such circumstances, the mediator should refuse to convey the offer as his suggestion and insist that it be conveyed by the party directly to the other side.

13 RECOMMENDATIONS BY MEDIATORS

Closely akin to offers and explorations is the problem of recommendations made by mediators at a joint meeting.

For a long time, it was a cardinal principle of good mediation that the only proper place for suggesting an alternative or compromise solution to an issue or issues in dispute was in a separate meeting. It was only in rare cases where the mediator departed from this rule.

Such suggestions or compromises were informal and made orally. No thought was ever given to formalizing such suggestions in writing. The publicizing of such suggestions was never even considered.

Many mediators felt that if a suggestion was formalized and publicized, it was stating in effect that in the mediator's opinion the suggestion represented his judgment as to what would be a fair and equitable solution to the dispute. If the suggestion was rejected by one or both parties, he would have lost his effectiveness thereafter. Further, if rejected, it ill behooved him a few days later to formalize another and different suggestion as to what would be a fair and equitable solution of the dispute.

Within the past five years, there has occurred a number of situations which have dictated the need for experimentation in the area of mediator's recommendations. A number of disputes have arisen which have resulted in extended stoppages. A study of some of these cases has revealed that the issues remaining in dispute did not warrant prolongation of the stoppage with its attendant impact on the employees, company and the economic welfare of the community. Yet either because of prior positions taken by the parties or because of political interplays, they were reluctant to change their bargaining posture. In other cases, each party felt that if it came forward with a compromise of its prior position on an issue, the move would be construed as a sign of weakness on its part. If so misconstrued, the other party instead of responding with a change of position would firm up and demand not compromise but surrender. In still other cases, the criticality to the national defense effort of the products produced was such that a stoppage of production was intolerable.

In all such cases and in similar cases, it appeared that it would be totally irresponsible to permit the dispute to continue without some affirmative action by the mediator beyond his utilization of persuasion and separate meeting suggestions. The public interest demanded a review of the traditional mediation policy.

Experiments were undertaken in highly selective cases. In 95% of the cases, both parties accepted the mediator's recommendations. In 3% of the cases, the recommendations were accepted by one party but rejected by the other. In the remainder of the cases, both parties rejected. As an interesting sidelight, a comparison of the terms of the final settlement and the recommendations in those cases where either or both parties rejected reveal that there were few, if any, variations.

To be effective, the mediation tool of recommendations should be infrequently used and then only in very selective cases.

The determination of what is a proper case for recommendations depends on whether the case meets the following criteria:

1. A threatened strike or the prolongation of an existing strike is having a major impact on the community involved, or the defense effort, or it has been attended by violence.

2. The parties are deadlocked and no negotiated solution appears possible in the immediate future.

3. The parties have rejected alternative methods of solving the issues.

4. The mediator has a thorough knowledge of the issues in dispute.

5. The mediator has, by judicious explorations in joint or separate conferences, obtained a "feeling" for the issues and believes a middle ground exists.

If a particular dispute meets these criteria, the mediator can go forward and make a suggestion or even a recommendation at the joint meeting specifically setting forth the possible solutions to the outstanding issues.

Before such presentation the mediator should advise the parties that unless they are able to find a solution themselves by a fixed time he will have to give serious consideration to the making of recommendations.

In some cases, the very existence of a threat of possible recommendations has been sufficient to inspire agreement.

In a number of these cases, these recommendations or suggestions have been reduced to writing and handed to the parties in each others' presence.

Generally mediators preface the written recommendation by:

(a) Recitation of the importance and impact of dispute.

(b) Recitation of the number of meetings held by the mediator in an attempt to help the parties resolve the dispute.

(c) The futility of such meetings.

(d) A statement that as long as the parties adhere to their present positions, no agreement appears possible in the immediate foreseeable future.

(e) That in light of these factors, he is proposing "at this time" the following solutions.

After the parties have received the copies of the document, the mediator should <u>not</u> permit any discussion as to the merits of the recommendations at that time and merely entertain questions relating solely to clarification.

If no such questions are asked, he should request the parties to study the recommendations in separate caucuses and advise him in a prescribed time of their acceptance or rejection.

If the making of recommendations is the course that the mediator decides to pursue, the question then arises as to whether he should make the recommendations public knowledge.

Each party to a labor contract negotiation is keenly conscious of its public relations position. Each is seeking to elicit public support for the alleged fairness and reasonableness of its offer or demand. At the minimum, each seeks sympathetic neutrality; at the maximum, each seeks the exertion of public pressure which will impel the other party to either accept the offer or demand or to modify its position.

Normally, neither party desires to have a public exposure by a neutral of the true differences between them. Nor, generally speaking, do they desire to have the public know that the neutral suggested a solution and they have rejected it.

Recognizing these facts, when mediators do make recommendations, in most cases, they will reserve the right to make such recommendations public.

Experience indicates that the mere threat to do so at a later day compels each party seriously to consider the recommendations and, if unacceptable in whole or in part, to reevaluate their position and find a new approach to the solution of the unresolved issues.

An examination of the disputes in which mediators have made recommendations shows that it has seldom been necessary to make the recommendations public. Apparently, they stimulated further thinking which led to a breaking of the log jam in the negotiations.

If the parties do accept the mediator's recommendations, the preferable practice is to announce publicly that recommendations have been made but not to disclose the specific terms pending the ratification meeting.

Length of Separate Conference or Caucus

The separate conference or caucus should continue until the mediator feels that the purpose for which it was called has been satisfied or that the deadlock has been broken so that further progress can be made by joint discussions.

There are times when one of the parties may adhere tenaciously to a bargaining goal which the mediator feels is unrealistic or impossible to achieve. The mediator may be further persuaded that unless that party abandons or substantially modifies his position, further progress will be impeded. Under such circumstances, despite the persuasiveness used by the mediator, that party, relying on some statement out of context, lack of emphasis or rumor, may persist in his position. In such situations the mediator may recess the separate conference and have the parties meet jointly so that the hopelessness of the position can be exposed firsthand.

Conferring With Other Side After Separate Conference

Whenever a mediator decides that he should terminate a separate conference with one party and resume joint discussions, he should make it a point first to confer briefly and separately with the other party.

There is an understandable curiosity on the part of the party who has been caucused as to what is transpiring while the mediator confers with the other. Further, he has a right to know what is the next step. If the mediator does not satisfy both desires, his next step will be viewed with suspicion and distrust.

14 MEETINGS GENERALLY

There are a number of guiding principles for a mediator to follow if he is to make the maximum contribution to the negotiations.

Timing

One of the keystones of successful mediation is timing. Timing escapes definition. It can only be acquired. It cannot be taught by rote, but only by experience. It becomes a sort of sixth sense which a good mediator consciously or unconsciously develops.

It can be described broadly as a sense a mediator develops as to when to urge a particular solution or approach which would have a maximum impact on negotiations and be most effective and acceptable. If a suggestion is made too soon, it may be rejected out of hand. If too late, it may be disregarded.

One of the mistakes most often committed by the inexperienced mediator is in this area. After a few meetings, such a mediator may discern a logical solution to a particular issue or a series of issues. His impatience, born often of immaturity in the field, will prompt him to urge its adoption vigorously. He is then a very disappointed young man when the parties summarily dismiss his brainchild.

In order for a mediator's suggestion to have the greatest weight, it must be made at a time when the parties have reached a stage in their negotiations at which they will be most receptive.

One of the prerequisites to receptivity is that the parties must have been conditioned to accept the less perfect because it may lead to an agreement, rather than to insist on the perfect which

only continues the impasse. This phase also has been characterized as the development of the consent to lose.

A true union committee reflects the hopes of the entire membership. Many times it is charged with the responsibility of vigorously bargaining for demands which many of the negotiating
committeemen know are impractical to achieve. Often a vociferous group representing a small segment of a plant will succeed
in incorporating as a "must" some demand which reflects solely
its special interests, regardless of its impact on the majority.
For a union officer or a committee to refuse to carry such demands to the bargaining table would jeopardize their political
position and, indeed, may endanger the union's representation
status. Consequently, the committee cannot abandon the issue
until it has made strenuous efforts to obtain it. After the committee has pressed for it without success, the membership may
then realize that concessions affecting the majority are being
denied because of the presence of these special interest issues.
At that point, they are receptive to a mediation suggestion.

Other times, based on some information or rumor, the union
or the management may feel that if a certain bargaining strategy
is followed, its aims can be achieved. Until they have pursued
this strategy and found it futile, any suggestion will fall on deaf
ears. Each side must have its run--until economic pressures
and realism take hold.

Presence of a Stenographer or Tape Recorder

There will be occasions where the mediator will be confronted
by the insistence of one party to agree to the presence of a tape
recorder or stenographer at the bargaining conferences.

Experience has taught that the presence of a stenographer
or tape recorder does inhibit free collective bargaining. Both
sides talk for the record and not for the purpose of advancing negotiations toward eventual settlement. Each becomes overcon-
scious of the recording of his remarks. The ease of expression
so necessary to proper exposition of problems is hampered. The
discussion generally becomes stultified.

If the past bargaining practice of the parties is to conduct
their negotiations in the presence of a tape recorder or stenographer,

there is little the mediator can do to exclude them. Similarly, if there is no past practice and both parties consent, the mediator must in main adapt himself to the bargaining pattern which both parties urge.

Even where both parties consent, the mediator should advise both parties of the roadblocks to free discussion occasioned by a recording. Further, he should point out that the confidentiality which surrounds mediation meetings is jeopardized. Under the rules, either statutory or administrative, of most mediation agencies, a mediator may not disclose what is conveyed to him during the course of his mediation efforts without the consent of the head of his agency. Because of the public policy considerations, such consent is seldom granted. A stenographic or tape recording of a mediation conference can be produced by either party at a judicial or administrative hearing without the safeguards of prior consent of the mediation agency. Under these circumstances, a mediator can be less effective.

Lengthy Meetings

A common picture often painted by lay writers is that of the mediator locking both parties in a room and keeping them there until, in a state of complete physical and mental exhaustion, they will agree to most anything in order to obtain their release.

This is one of the most nonsensical and vicious myths ever perpetuated on the general public. It visualizes a mediator who has no home, no need for normal rest or recreation, a physical specimen who can out-endure men often 10 or 15 years his junior, and capable of physically and legally preventing the participants from breaking off negotiations whenever they desire to do so.

Mediators in the main are middle-aged or older with all the concomitant physical disabilities. They are normal individuals who enjoy their homes and families. They seek normal eating periods. They require reasonable rest and recreation. They certainly would enjoy a quiet evening at home much more than listening to parties repeat their positions ad nauseam, usually in a hot and eye-smarting smoke-filled room.

The truth of the matter is that in almost all incidents of all night or marathon continuous bargaining sessions, the mediator has had to adapt himself to a bargaining pattern followed by the parties for many a year. Traditionally and historically, many parties feel that no agreement is possible unless and until they have indulged in at least one of such sessions. Perhaps political considerations dictate such a course of conduct but seldom, if ever, is it inspired by the mediator.

A typical example comes to mind. In the New York area, year after year, the mediators assigned to a dispute found that the bargaining session on the eve of the termination of the contract would inevitably last from 10:00 a.m. to 6:30 a.m. the next morning. A pattern emerged--the company would withhold its final offer until 11:50 p.m. On the receipt of the offer, the union would call for a caucus agreeing that for deadline purposes, the clock was stopped as long as negotiations were continuous. Inevitably the union caucus continued until 6:00 a.m. at which time the union would announce acceptance of the offer with very inconsequential modifications. A half-hour joint conference would quickly dispose of these requested changes. The usual handshaking and self-pitying remarks would follow.

After several mediators had been subjected to this type of bargaining and had compared notes, it was discovered that the only reason why the union committee kept its caucus in session until 6:00 a.m. was the belief on its part that the only way the union membership would accept the offer and re-elect them was for the committee to appear at the plant at 8:00 a.m., when the first shift reported, with bloodshot eyes, bewhiskered chins, rumpled collars, and tousled hair. They could then loudly proclaim how they worked all night--as evidenced by their physical appearance--to obtain the contract improvements for the rank and file. The time between 6:30 a.m. and 8:00 a.m. was to permit the committee members to eat hearty breakfasts (at union expense) and travel to the plant.

Parenthetically, after this discovery, the mediator's no-sleep problem was practically solved by mediator's designating an office with a couch as the mediator's conference room.

Backtracking

In cases where there is a multiplicity of issues and protracted negotiations, there may arise serious questions between the parties as to whether an issue or series of issues have been withdrawn or tentatively settled. If tentatively settled, the question may further arise as to what disposition was made of such issue or issues. Resort to notes may not prove helpful because under the normal tensions of collective bargaining conferences, notes are often inadequate, sketchy or contradictory.

Where this situation arises, backtracking becomes inevitable which can only prolong and worsen the dispute. Equally disrupting are the emotional reactions evoked since questions of veracity come to the fore.

There are a number of devices which a mediator can suggest which are calculated to avoid or minimize the problem of backtracking.

Whenever a meeting is about to adjourn, if there have been some tentative agreements reached, ideally the parties should reduce such agreements to writing. Such memoranda should set forth in simplified general terms the agreements reached. No attempt should be made to draft precise contract language.

If it is impractical to reduce the agreed items to writing at the end of each session, the parties should orally summarize at a joint meeting the general nature of the tentative agreement or agreements. If there are any misunderstandings, they can be quickly resolved since the matters are still fresh in the minds of the participants.

While not directly related to mediation, it might be profitable to mention a device used in some sections of the United States to avoid misunderstandings of the application of formal contract language. It is the practice of explanatory addenda to the agreement. The addenda is cast in the form of a series of examples of the application of a particular section or subsection of the agreement. It is particularly applicable to sections relating to distribution of overtime, work overlapping regularly scheduled shifts, reporting pay, bumping sequence in seniority provisions and the like.

A typical example of this approach would be a contract providing the employees required to work prior to their regularly scheduled shift shall receive time-and-a-half for all hours worked prior thereto and also provided for shift differentials for the second and third shift. The addendum would set forth an example as follows:

If Employee A, receiving a rate of $3.00 per hour, is regularly scheduled on the first shift and is called in one hour before the start of the first shift and works through the first shift, he shall receive:

$$
\begin{aligned}
\text{1 hour at \$4.50 (\$3.00 plus 1 1/2 times)} &= \$\ 4.50 \\
\text{8 hours at \$3.00} &= \underline{\ 24.00} \\
&\ \ \ \$28.50
\end{aligned}
$$

Transmission of Final Offer

The proper transmission of the employer's final offer, especially if it culminates in agreement, is quite important to a mediator.

The cardinal principle is that no mediator should convey a final offer if he has been shuttling between the parties during separate conferences unless he reconvenes the parties in a joint meeting and repeats the offer in the presence of both.

This procedure eliminates any possibility of misunderstanding. If there is any doubt as to the meaning or import of the offer, it can be clarified then and there. Neither party can thereafter raise a question that the mediator did not properly transmit the offer.

15 LAST OFFER BALLOT VOTE

Quite often management representatives will insist that the mediator compel the union to "comply with the law" and submit the company's last offer to secret ballot vote on the union membership. This insistence, apart from its wisdom as good bargaining strategy, is often based on a misconception of the law.

Section 203(c) of the Labor-Management Relations Act, as amended, provides:

> "If the Director is not able to bring the parties to agreement by conciliation within a reasonable time, he shall seek to induce the parties voluntarily to seek other means of settling the dispute without resort to strike, lock-out, or other coercion, including submission to the employees in the bargaining unit of the employer's last offer of settlement for approval or rejection in a secret ballot. The failure or refusal of either party to agree to any procedure suggested by the Director shall not be deemed a violation of any duty or obligation imposed by this Act."

As indicated by the quoted statutory language, the mediator, as a representative of the Director of the Service, has the duty to induce the parties to seek methods other than mediation of settling the dispute but--

(a) the method suggested must be voluntarily accepted by the parties;

(b) if either or both fail or refuse to accept such procedure, they cannot be charged with any violation of the Act.

If the suggested procedure is the submission of the last offer to a secret ballot, the first difficulty is that the union is free to accept or reject it and there are no legal sanctions which could compel acceptance of the suggestions.

The decision as to acceptance or rejection of the last offer ballot procedure by a union representative is based often on very practical consideration. Bear in mind that the suggestion would only be made after the union representative and the negotiating committee have rejected the employer's last offer as being unresponsive to the demands of the union membership. The judgment of the union negotiators as to the acceptability of the last offer may or may not have solid foundation in fact. The important thing is that the union negotiators have taken a position before the company negotiators. If they feel that the offer has any possibility of being accepted, they will not agree to submit it since they would be placed in a poor light in future negotiations because of the doubt as to whether they are truly reflective of the desires of the membership. If the union negotiators feel that the offer will be rejected, then they may readily agree. A rejection will strengthen their bargaining position and if the employer desires a prompt settlement he must start from the plateau of his last offer and substantially improve it.

There are further difficulties. The statute makes no provision for a neutral supervision of the conduct and count of the secret ballot. The union is well within its statutory rights to insist that it and it alone will arrange, conduct and count the balloting.

It is interesting to note that if the last offer ballot procedure is suggested, a union may impose conditions which would make a company hastily reconsider its insistence on it. In a recent dispute involving one of the major manufacturing companies in the nation, the company urged the union to submit its last offer to the membership on the ground that it felt reasonably certain that its employeee would recognize the soundness and fairness of its offer and accept it overwhelmingly. The union stated that it was perfectly willing to do so--in fact would even consent to have an outside agency supervise and conduct the secret ballot and it would

69

abide by the result. It stated, however, that since the company's suggestion called into question whether the union was faithfully mirroring the desires of the employees, the ballot should also include the union's last demands so that the employees could choose between both. Of course, the union stated, it would expect the company to agree that it also would be bound by the results of the balloting. The company reconsidered its request.

There is difficulty, too, as to what is a final offer. If final refers to point of time, there is no problem. However, if final connotes an end position, the concept becomes fluid. What may be a final offer at one point of negotiations may become merely a preliminary or intermediate offer later as the exigencies of the bargaining change.

Eve of Strike Public Relations Problems

On the eve of an inevitable strike, the mediator should be particularly sensitive to the attempts by each party to embark on the strike in the most favorable public relations position.

Apart from public appeals through the press, the parties may suggest procedures for the settlement of the dispute even though they know in advance of the suggestions that they are unacceptable to the other party. In most cases these suggested procedures, such as arbitration, fact-finding and the like, are advanced solely for public relations reasons.

The mediator is faced with a problem when one of the parties requests that he be the vehicle of transmission. While he certainly has a duty to induce the parties to voluntarily seek other means of settling the dispute without resort to strike or lock-out, and such "other means" encompasses arbitration and fact-finding, he may become the unwitting tool of one of the parties and thereby destroy his future effectiveness. It is not the mediator's function to enhance the public relations position of one party at the expense of the other.

The better mediation practice would appear to be for the mediator, in response to his statutory duty, to explore the alternate procedures with each party separately to see if they present any hope of achievement. This practice will disclose the practicality or futility of urging their adoption at a joint meeting. If one of

70

the parties insists that it be broached at a joint meeting, the counsel of wisdom dictates that the mediator in turn insist that the
moving party make it his offer and present it directly at the joint
bargaining session.

There is, of course, the larger question as to the efficacy
of the force of public opinion in the average labor dispute. Whether, in such cases, the efforts to marshall public opinion into
fruitful and persuasive channels are worthwhile can be the subject
of a rather extensive research project.

16 AGREEMENT AIDS

There are a number of approaches which mediators, as well as negotiators, have found helpful in overcoming roadblocks to agreement which often occur in the course of negotiations. Some of these have been treated in the suggestions made concerning the conduct of joint and separate meetings. It may be profitable to allude to a few additional approaches.

1. "No."

Many times during negotiations, a mediator's suggestion or transmittal of an offer is met with an unequivocal, flat rejection --expressed by a simple "no." It is axiomatic that there cannot be any hope of changing the inflexibility of a flat "No." It seems to preclude any further discussion. However, if the party urging that "No" can be persuaded to state the reasons which led to his negative conclusion, persuasion and flexibility may be restored. An alert mediator would therefore seek out the reasons and then analyze and examine them in the light of the problem under discussion. By such exposure, the soundness of the flat conclusion may be reappraised. If the reasons fail to sustain the ultimate negative, the negative itself may become untenable and the roadblock to further progress overcome.

2. "You."

It is an old sales principle that you buy an article not because someone is selling it but rather because you feel, rightly or wrongly, that you need it. A good salesman always seeks to instill into the prospect this sense of need. Once established, the sale can be readily made.

The same basic technique applies to collective bargaining. If the offer or counterproposal is presented not as a demand but rather as a solution to a need, it becomes more readily susceptible of acceptance. Good collective bargaining is basically a solving of problems of mutual interest. If an offer or counterproposal appears to solve a problem of one of the parties, he is much more amenable.

The value of the "you" approach was clearly illustrated in a Teamster negotiations that occurred several years ago on the Eastern seaboard. One of the chief objectives of the union was the establishment of a pension plan. If the union presented it as a bargaining "must", it would have been quickly rejected. The chief union negotiator, however, pointed to the low productivity record of the large number of superannuated employees in the industry and the need for the industry to achieve greater productivity if it desired to maintain its financial and competitive position. Younger employees were needed. At the same time, simple justice required recognition of the long and faithful service rendered the industry by the old timers. After vividly painting the picture and conditioning the industry to the problem it faced, the union suggested as a possible solution of the industry's problem a pension plan. It argued that it would solve the problem of productivity by permitting the company to introduce younger workers in the industry as replacements for the "old timers" who could be retired with dignity and financial security. This approach led to the establishment of the pension program.

3. "Representative Cloak"

Many of us will seek shelter behind our title or position when we desire to divorce our decision-making from our individual feelings and thinking. We often hear the remark that as an individual the suggested course of action appears just, but as the vice president of the company or the business representative of the union it cannot be adopted. In effect, the speaker has thrown about him his representative cloak and speaks not as an individual but as a representative of another self-interest.

Mediators often experience this phenomenon during the course of negotiations. Even though the proposal being considered would tend to correct an injustice, the responsibility of being in a representative capacity will compel the other party to reject it.

If the proposal can be advanced in terms that will pierce the representative cloak and appeal to the individual, it will meet with greater receptivity.

A fair illustration would be a situation involving a request for call-in pay. The company representative as such representative may resist the demand because of the increase in costs which its granting may entail. In a desire to keep costs at a minimum, such a representative may overlook the human relations injustices which may be inherent in the denial of the request. By suggesting that he place himself in the shoes of the individual employee who leaves his home expecting work and who undergoes the inconvenience and expense of travel only to be told that, through no fault of his own, and not because of any Act of God, there is no work for him, the problem is brought home to that representative not as a representative but as an individual human being. As an individual he certainly would resent the injustice of it.

4. The Recalcitrant Committeeman

Several years ago, in a midwest aerospace negotiation, because of the multiplicity of issues and the imminency of the contract expiration date, the mediator decided that the most expeditious approach was to utilize a subcommittee. With the consent of the parties, such a subcommittee was established and two issues were divorced from the main table and placed in the jurisdiction of the selected subcommittee. When the union subcommittee subsequently reported the progress it was making, one member of the union bargaining committee who had not been selected to serve on the subcommittee vigorously opposed any of the subcommittee's suggested concessions.

Time and again, each time the subcommittee reported, the same individual succeeded in thwarting a possible compromise which would have led to a disposition of the issue entrusted to the subcommittee.

Faced with this roadblock to the progress of negotiations, the mediator resorted to the technique which is founded on the pedestrian advice--"if you can't lick them, join them." He suggested that the subcommittee be expanded by one member from each side and, with the assistance of the chief union negotiator, made certain that the recalcitrant committeeman was one of those selected.

After this move, the negotiating climate changed dramatically. During the subcommittee's deliberations, the recalcitrant was most conciliatory and was in the forefront of those suggesting accommodations which led to the disposition of the issue.

Often, failure to include a certain union committeeman in the across-the-table dialogue or on subcommittees may prove to be the obstacle to agreement. It is human to desire recognition. This becomes especially true as far as members of the negotiating committee are concerned. Such committeemen are proud of the fact that their fellow workers have elected or selected them over all others as their spokesman. If during the course of the negotiations they are led to believe that they and their opinions are being ignored by the other committeemen, they become resentful. The only outlet available to them to demonstrate their frustration is to force recognition by opposing what their colleagues are doing.

If such a situation is presented, mediators may do well to consider the possible advantage of having the recalcitrant more closely identified with the dialogue and the structuring of the final settlement.

17 BEAR TRAPS FOR MEDIATORS

There are several situations to which a new mediator may be subject which if not properly met may cause difficulties in his attempts effectively to assist the parties to a dispute. These have been termed "bear traps."

1. Fair Offer

Quite often during the course of a joint meeting, a company or union representative, after extolling the justness and fairness of his proposal, will state: "I will leave it to the mediator's judgment whether or not it is a fair and good proposal." A silence follows as both sides gaze down to the head of the table awaiting anxiously the mediator's reply.

In such situations, if the mediator responds in either the affirmative or negative he is tarnishing his image as the neutral. Yet a response is expected.

At this moment, the real question is not what is a fair, just or equitable offer but rather what is an acceptable offer. The mediator's evaluation as to the merits of the offer is really immaterial. Consequently, the mediator should refuse to give his own appraisal of the offer at the joint conference and indicate to the inquirer that the determinative opinion as to fairness and justness is not his but that of the other party.

When conducting separate conferences, however, the mediator may and often does express his opinion as to the relative merits of an offer or counterproposal in light of other area and industry settlements.

2. Conditional Meetings

Quite often when a mediation meeting has in the judgment of one party been particularly unproductive, the disappointed party may insist that the mediator not schedule any further meetings unless he has prior assurance that the other party is ready to change its position. In a few instances, the condition imposed on further meetings is that the other party be prepared to meet the last stated position.

To permit either party to impose preconditions on further meetings is to thwart any possibility of a settlement. Even though, because of economic pressures or other circumstances, one party may be placed in the position of having to accede to the other's demands, it would be bargaining folly to attend a meeting with a pre-conference commitment of surrender. Such a posture not only invites the interjection of new issues but is also destructive of future bargaining relationships. A surrender to such ultimata in the present negotiations will encourage similar threats in the future.

Mediators should remember that a conference scheduled and conducted by a mediator is his conference and not that of the parties. Further, the mediator is carrying forward a statutory responsibility in the public interest. Consequently, neither party has a right to dictate preconditions to the scheduling of any mediation conference.

Faced with this situation, the mediator should reject the suggestion and advise the parties that, in fulfillment of his statutory responsibility, he and he alone will determine when and under what conditions a further meeting will be scheduled. The onus of refusing to attend with its consequent effect on that party's constituency and public relations posture is placed upon the party insisting on the preconditions.

3. Legal Opinions

Many mediators either have a background in law, or were formerly associated with a state or federal regulatory agency concerned with wages and hours, labor relations, minimum wages and such like.

77

During the course of some negotiations, a question of the legality of a demand or offer may arise. If the parties have knowledge of the mediator's background or prior affiliations, they may solicit his opinion.

Unless the inquiry is directly related to the mediation statute or regulation under which the mediator is functioning, it is imprudent for him to give an opinion on the legality of the matter before the parties. Even though the mediator thinks he knows the answer, he is treading on dangerous ground. Statutes are subject to amendment and rules and regulations issued thereunder are subject to change. Unless one specializes in a particular subject as part of his daily duties, it is almost impossible to keep abreast of the recurring changes in the act or interpretations thereof. The advice given may well be outdated.

Further, parties normally have ready access to legal counsel. It is the responsibility of such counsel and not of the mediator to properly advise his client.

If the mediator believes that a demand, offer or suggested compromise may be of doubtful legality, he has a duty to raise the question and to suggest that before the parties proceed on that issue they seek legal counsel. If despite his admonition the parties desire to go forward without obtaining the suggested advice, the mediator should not deter them.

4. Bargaining in Good Faith

In circumstances quite similar to that described in "fair offer," a mediator may be confronted at a joint meeting by a demand that he pass judgment on the good faith bargaining of one side or the other. This demand is usually proceeded by across the table accusation of bad faith.

Whether a party is or is not bargaining in good faith is not a matter for a determination of the mediator. His sole responsibility is to assist the parties to resolve the issues separating them. The meeting he has scheduled is designed to accomplish that purpose and not be a judicial or quasi-judicial forum for determining the bona fides of one party or the other.

Usually, the question is a rhetorical one. No direct answer is expected. The better practice would be for the mediator to ignore the question and suggest that the parties pass on to another issue.

If the inquirer is persistent and presses for an answer, then the mediator should advise him of the purpose for which the meeting was called. He should also advise that, if the inquirer desires to pursue his accusation, there is another forum (either the national or state labor relations board) to which he has recourse for a determination.

5. Instructed Committee

There will be occasions where a mediator will be confronted with an alleged instructed committee.

Illustrative of such a situation is the case where the mediator has scheduled a conference. Prior to jointly convening the parties, the union committee advises the mediator that at a membership meeting held a few days previously the union membership mandated the committee to settle for 25¢ an hour increase and therefore, unless the employer is prepared to meet that exact figure, there will be no point to continuing the mediation meeting. Obviously, if the union committee maintains this posture, meaningful negotiations are impossible. There are several approaches which have been utilized by mediators to avoid the consequences of a committee maintaining this position.

The first approach is an appeal to the pride of the individual committee members. The mediator can point out that the membership apparently has no faith in the judgment of the negotiating committee or else they would have placed some discretion in them. Further, he can stress that the union membership should not have bothered even going through the charade of electing or selecting a negotiating committee when a Western Union messenger boy could have served the function the committee was asked to perform.

If the appeal to pride does not break down the mandated posture, then a mediator may try the technique of the "false crisis." This is accomplished by first highlighting the position of the committee. It has been done by the following dialogue:

> Mediator--"Let me understand your position quite clearly. You say that the membership has mandated you to get 25¢ an hour?"

> Committee Chairman--"That is correct."

Mediator--"In a word that means that even if the
employer was to offer you 24 9/10¢ you would reject it because of your mandate?"

Often the mediator need not go further. The exposure of the
ridiculousness of the union's position leads to a union caucus and
an abandonment of their mandated position.

If, however, the committee adheres to its position, the mediator can state that there is really no point to prolonging the proceedings and suggest that the parties immediately meet jointly so
that the employer can hear directly from the committee as to the
mandate. The mediator also announces that if the employer rejects the demand, he will adjourn the meeting without date and
see if he can fit in the next meeting in two or three weeks.

This technique often creates a "crisis." The union committee now realizes that it can expect a resounding "no" from the
employer's representatives and that the joint meeting would be
of only a few minutes duration with the prospects of a further
meeting two or three weeks away. Their report to the membership becomes a weighty responsibility. Despite their selection as
the negotiators for the membership, they are faced with the prospect of having nothing to report except a demand and an out-of-
hand rejection. They are not in a position to report explorations,
counteroffers or arguments.

In almost every case, the union committee caucuses and then
authorizes the mediator to proceed in the normal manner.

6. Contract Drafting and Signing

The normal practice after a tentative agreement has been ratified is for the company representative or attorney to draft the
new contract. When the draft has been prepared, the parties often
meet jointly to go over the proposed language and, if satisfactory,
to sign the contract.

Most mediators will avoid attending such meetings. Quite
often, when the parties are discussing the draft language, questions
arise as to whether the proposed language correctly reflects the
understandings reached at the bargaining table. Most of the objections raised are of a minor nature and are quickly resolved by
the parties themselves.

If a mediator attends such a meeting, the parties may use him as a crutch and the issues raised devolve into a question of credibility. The mediator is then placed in a position of an arbiter of truth or falsity. As a result, his future acceptability may be injured.

Of course, if the disagreement is of a major nature, then the mediator has a duty to assist the parties to resolve their differences.

In the normal case, the mediator's responsibility should terminate when the tentative agreement has been ratified. The drafting and execution of the formal contract is the responsibility of the parties. It is their duty to reflect correctly the understandings and to couch them in language which makes their day-to-day application practical.

7. Attendance at Union Membership Meetings

Mediators, on occasion, have been invited to attend ratification meetings. Usually, they are urged to do so on the basis of assisting the negotiating committee to explain and "sell" the package which has been tentatively agreed to by the committee.

Except in an exceptional case, mediators decline such invitations. The reason is that the ratification process is normally an internal union affair into which the mediator should not physically intrude. Over and beyond this basic reason is the question of responsibility. The basic responsibility for "selling" the package belongs to the committee, not the mediator. They, and not he, were selected by their fellow members to represent them and to bring back any agreement reached with their comments.

There are, however, times when circumstances dictate the mediator's presence at the meeting. In such circumstances, there are two cautions which should be observed:

a. Never be the first speaker. This caution is born of bitter experience. There have been instances in which the mediator permitted himself to be called on first to extol the virtues of the tentative agreement. At the conclusion of his remarks, a dissident minority registered its disapproval by shouts and stamping of feet. Fearing similar treatment, each following speaker

81

refused to carry out his commitment to recommend the settlement or else did so in a most unenthusiastic manner. The mediator was left alone in an embarrassing position and his future usefulness in that dispute seriously impaired.

The mediator should insist that the negotiating committee take the platform first. If they fail to endorse the tentative agreement, he should decline to speak.

b. <u>Never characterize the offer as to its fairness and justness.</u> Since the acceptance or rejection of the offer is dependent on its acceptability, the mediator should not impose upon the membership his own judgment as to its fairness or justness. The mediator should confine his remarks to explaining the offer, to paying tribute to the integrity and hard work of the negotiating committee and to indicating that the offer was the best that could be obtained at that time, and if appropriate, without a lengthy and costly stoppage.

If the mediator goes beyond the suggested limitations, he will, in the event of a rejection, be hard put to justify his actions in trying to get an improvement in an offer which he has publicly stated is fair and just.

18 MEMBERSHIP REJECTIONS OF RECOMMENDED SETTLEMENTS-- TECHNIQUES FOR MINIMIZING

One of the more disturbing problems negotiators encounter in present-day bargaining is the high incident of rejection of recommended tentative agreements by the union membership.

The situation referred to is one in which the duly elected or selected union negotiating committee and the representatives of the employer have reached an understanding across the bargaining table, and the union committee has stated that it would recommend it to the membership for acceptance. The union committee honestly and sincerely carries out its commitment at the membership meeting and, despite its action, the membership rejects the settlement.

This type situation first came to the attention of the Federal Mediation and Conciliation Service in 1964 when it noticed that in 8.7% of the cases in which it was involved, tentative agreements were rejected by the membership.

Subsequent events proved that this was not a phenomena which was characteristic of some special economic problem peculiar to that year. The rate of rejections climbed steadily until it reached a peak of over 14% in 1967. In 1968, it dropped to 11%. Everyone then thought that the problem would soon dissipate. This proved to be a false hope; the rate of rejections began to rise again, and it now exceeds 12%.

This study of the Federal Mediation and Conciliation Service was confined to the approximately 7,500 cases in which that Service participated. It did not include disputes which were handled exclusively by state and local mediation agencies. Further, it did not include multiple rejections. The latter type of rejection involves situations where in the same set of negotiations the union membership rejects the recommended settlement two or more times. In the area of multiple rejections, the Service conducted

83

a limited survey of 1,563 cases and found that in 21% of these cases, tentative agreements had been rejected two or more times before the agreement was ratified.

Whether the inclusion of the state and local mediation agencies' experience and the cases of multiple rejections would increase or decrease over the 12% rate of rejections must, of course, be speculative. Generally speaking, it is doubtful whether the inclusion of these disputes would significantly change it.

If nothing is done to minimize the chances of a rejection, it will not only lead to an unhealthy instability in negotiations but it is also destructive of the unity and leadership which makes a union an effective and respected spokesman for the betterment of the economic conditions of the rank and file members.

When a union submits a set of demands to an employer, that employer has a right to feel that those demands reflect the desires of his employees. He also has the right to believe that if he meets those demands, either by concession or compromise, and obtains the agreement of the selected or elected union bargaining agreement, he has an agreement. If the membership rejects it, he has every right to question seriously whether the union spokesman or his committee really do represent his employees. Equally disturbing is the fact that his faith in the leadership abilities of the union representative will be destroyed.

There have been many theories advanced as to the causes of such rejections.

One of the earliest theories was that the union leadership image was destroyed by the disclosures of the McClellan investigation. This theory does not appear very tenable. While the derelictions of some union leaders and their reckless disregard for their responsibilities to the rank and file were publicly exposed and did shake the confidence of some union members in their elected officials, it was also evident that the malfeasances and misfeasances were confined to a very insignificant minority of union leaders.

When union leaders are questioned as to the cause, many point to the impact of the Landrum-Griffin Act. They allege that the control which they could exercise over dissident groups has been greatly weakened by the Act and that any attempt by the International to exercise sanctions, such as trusteeship and the like, are fraught with legal technicalities and the possibilities of damage suits.

Failure of union leaders to evaluate properly the desires and aspirations of the rank and file member is also cited as a cause. For a long period of time, negotiators on both sides of the table have become so engrossed in the main issues that they have swept aside, without resolution, so-called peripheral local issues. They have often described these local issues as nuisances which could be withdrawn or submerged by the size of the economic pie being offered. What they apparently fail to realize is that a grievance (and many of the so-called local issues are really that), which is not corrected, can fester and grow out of all proportion to the original complaint. Local issues are close to the rank and file member. Generally, they involve his day-to-day working relationship and are directly and personally related to him. Pensions, health and welfare improvements are appreciated by an employee but usually only when circumstances compel him to resort to them. Normally there is no immediacy to them. Violations, real or fancied, of his seniority rights, unsettled grievances, improper classifications, the over-aggressive foreman who insists on a too rigid compliance with the labor agreement are problems which confront him daily. They are constant irritants.

Another theory that has been advanced as a probable reason for the high rate of rejections is the failure of labor leaders to exercise the responsibility which enures to their position as leaders. Those who espouse this theory state that positions in International Unions have become so desirable both from a monetary and status viewpoint that the incumbents have become too job-security conscious. They allege that the average labor leader will avoid a conflict with local leaders of rank and file in order to assure his political future, even though the local leadership or a particular rank and file group seek goals which may be detrimental to the economic existence of the industry or company involved. It is much easier for such leaders to follow than to take a strong position.

Some commentators in the academic field point to the upward trend in the educational level of the average American worker which impels him to question more closely the judgment of his representatives. The median educational level of the American worker is 12.5 years of school. Completing of high school is 12. Those who espouse this theory point out that many times in the past, the rank and file member might defer because of his lack of

education to the recommendations of his local business representative or International officer. Now he feels that such representatives no longer have a corner on wisdom; he feels they are at
least equals.

Another reason advanced for the high rate of rejections is the
unsatisfactory and inadequate communications. It is a typical
practice to keep the results of negotiations secret until the union
leader and the committee make their report to the membership.
As a result, there may be too great a gap between the members'
expectations and the final settlement. Somehow or other union
leadership must bridge the gap between publicly stated objectives
and the settlement and the vote on ratification. The period may
be too short if it provides an inadequate opportunity to persuade
the membership to accept; it may be too long if it permits intra-
union politics to become operative.

And last, there are many who claim that this trend is another
manifestation of the revolt almost of worldwide proportions by the
younger element of our society against the "establishment."

Whether this phenomena can be attributed to one of these
causes or a combination of two or more could be the subject of
an interesting academic exercise.

To the practitioner, however, the more important consideration is what techniques to employ to minimize the possibility of a
rejection.

There are a number of techniques that can be suggested which,
if properly utilized in appropriate cases, can go a long way toward
narrowing the possibility of a rejection.

1. Greater Use of Subcommittees in Bargaining

The possibility of rejection can be minimized by greater utilization of subcommittees in the bargaining process. All too often
one or two of the principals go off by themselves and negotiate out
the proposed agreement. In such situations, the balance of the
committees usually sits in another room doing nothing. If there
is ever a situation which can engender suspicion and distrust, this
is certainly it.

Some may argue that this is not a very realistic approach.
Any experienced negotiator knows progress cannot be made where
there are large committees present, since everybody is talking

86

for the record. They won't let their hair down and really come to grips with the problems raised in the negotiations.

I am not advocating the abolishment of this time-proven agreement-making device. In fact, experience is that the vast majority of contracts have been reached through such an approach.

The subcommittee approach is something over and beyond the top level off-record meeting. During the course of most negotiations, issues arise which can be more expeditiously handled by divorcing them from the main bargaining table and permitting a subcommittee to explore possible solutions. Seniority, insurance, pensions and the like are usually fruitful issues for the subcommittee approach.

How can this device minimize the possibility of a rejection? It does so by assuring that each member of the negotiating committee participate in the structuring of the final settlement. It is only human for someone who has been singled out by his union brothers to want, to use the parlance of the day, "a piece of the action." If he is given the opportunity to become actively engaged in the across-the-table give and take, there is every assurance he will support the tentative agreement which is eventually arrived at by the parties.

2. Making Final Offer Contingent on a Recommendation

In presenting a final offer, management representatives should make it contingent on a recommendation of acceptance. This normally involves the company final offer being put before the committee on a basis that it must be recommended by the committee unanimously or else there is no offer before it. All too often mediators have witnessed company representatives who have been deluded into thinking that, if an offer is brought before the membership on either a split committee recommendation or presented without recommendation for or against, it will be accepted by the membership.

Experience has taught us that acceptance under these circumstances is a rare and unusual occurrence and that the possibilities of rejection are greatly increased when the final offer is presented by a split committee or without any recommendation whatsoever.

3. Entire Union Committee Should Make Commitment

This problem arises when it becomes apparent that one or more members of the union committee are political fence straddlers. During the course of negotiations they studiously avoid vocalizing their feelings. When the committee is planning its strategy, they neither agree nor disagree. When a tentative agreement is reached, they are noncommittal. When the membership meeting is called, they sniff the political winds. If they feel that ratification is doubtful, they will loudly proclaim that they had nothing to do with the tentative agreement; in fact, they were opposed to it. If the membership appears to be satisfied with the terms of the tentative agreement, they will insist that they were the only members of the negotiating committee who were solely responsible for the "goodies" in the package.

There is an effective way of dealing with this situation. Each and every member of the committee should be polled to ascertain whether they will join with the others in recommending the agreement. While this will not preclude individuals from taking a contrary position at the membership meeting, it will make it more difficult for them to do so and subject them to accusations of bad faith. At the very least, they cannot state that they did not agree with the settlement and had no part of it.

If it can be prearranged, the most desirable method is to have the poll conducted by the union spokesman; however, there appears to be no great obstacle to having the mediator or company representative doing it.

In conducting the poll, the union committee members who have openly stated their support of the tentative agreement should be polled first and those whom the negotiators feel are the "fence straddlers" last. If a majority of the committee have openly indicated their support, there is a psychological pressure on the remaining members to join with that majority.

4. Union's Avoidance of Announced Fixed Goals

Generally speaking, experience has demonstrated that union negotiators should avoid announcing a fixed bargaining goal either before or during early negotiations. This is particularly true in the wage area. If the committee announces a fixed wage increase goal, it may become a magic figure in the minds of the rank and file. If negotiations produce a smaller figure, the disappointment of the membership is heightened, and the possibility of a rejection increased.

Many union negotiators are keenly aware of this danger. They try to set a flexible goal, usually couched in terms of a "substantial increase." This permits the committee either to stress the magnitude of the wage increase obtained or the size of the total package, whichever is greater, at the membership meeting, and avoid the psychological block of a fixed wage goal.

5. Converting Last Offer to Union Offer

Wherever possible convert the employer's last offer to a union offer. If negotiations can be so guided that the union negotiating committee is placed in the position of making a final offer and the company accepting it, a deterrent to a rejection can be provided. Under such circumstances, the onus is on the union committee to persuade the membership to buy the package since it was the union's package to which the company acceded.

This technique can be more easily employed if the services of a mediator are utilized. The mediator, having advanced knowledge of the company's last offer, can, without disclosing it, indicate to the union committee that if they recase their demands in the framework of what he knows to be the company's last offer he will try to persuade the company to accede to it.

6. Reduction of Tentative Agreement to Writing

When oral agreement has been reached at the bargaining table, it should if possible be reduced to writing. This does not mean that it should be done with the drafting precision of final contract language, but it should outline the general terms of understanding.

After the agreement has been drafted, each member of the union committee should be requested to initial the instrument. In such an agreement there should be a sentence that the undersigned members of the union committee agree unanimously to recommend acceptance. (Such agreements should, of course, provide that they are being executed subject to ratification.) Again, this device will minimize the possibilities of one or two members of the committee denying before a membership body that they have agreed to the tentative agreement.

7. Use of Press Statements

There are occasions when after an exhausting negotiating session the parties have neither the patience nor the time to await the reduction of the tentative agreement to writing. Under such circumstances, the parties should consider the use of a joint press statement as a deterrent device to a possible rejection.

While, normally, such a release would not disclose the precise terms of the tentative agreement, it would announce the conclusion that a tentative agreement had been reached. It then should be followed by a statement, if such was the fact, that "the agreement will be unanimously recommended by the union negotiating committee consisting of (names of each member of the committee)." Any member of that committee who decides to backtrack would be embarrassed to do so at the membership meeting.

8. Committee Authorized to Make Final Agreement

One of the often-heard suggestions is predicated on having the union negotiating team fully authorized to conclude an agreement, and thus obviating the necessity for a ratification meeting. The argument for this position is that, in the normal case, the management team comes to the bargaining table fully authorized to make a binding agreement, and its counterpart should have equal authority.

This suggestion presents several difficulties. First, in many unions this flies in the teeth of union constitution and by-laws which spell out the requirement of a ratification meeting. Secondly, even in those cases where there is no union constitutional prohibition, it will violate long-established tradition, which would be destructive of the bargaining relationship. Lastly, it will deny the sense of participation by the rank and file in the decision-making process and may very well lead to their dissatisfaction with the terms of the new contract.

Perhaps a more palatable approach would be to have an official grouping larger than the negotiating committee but substantially smaller than the membership. This larger group would ratify or reject, and no further membership meeting would be required. This technique has been used rather successfully in multi-plant and multi-company bargaining. Query: could it be adaptable to a one-plant or one-company situation?

9. Contract Expiration Dates and Union Elections

Burton Zorn, who was one of the prominent employer attorneys, in a speech made at the Human Relations and Industry Conference, suggested that "Employers should try to set contract expiration dates (if other economic factors permit) at some reasonable time subsequent to the date of the local union election. It is true that competing candidates will out-promise each other, but this is a lesser evil than an expiration date before a union election, when the opposition candidates just will not agree on a reasonable settlement, or will continue a strike until the election has been held." This idea has merit.

Mediator's Involvement in Ratification Process

For a long number of years, the Federal Mediation and Conciliation Service, as well as management, adopted the policy that the mechanics of the union ratification process were purely an internal union affair and consequently the Service should play a minimal role.

The recent trend toward a comparatively high incidence of rejections has compelled the Service to reassess its position. Specifically, the Service urged its mediators to become more involved in the ratification process. Mediators were urged to counsel and advise union representatives in matters such as manner of presentation of a tentative agreement, the planning and conduct of the membership meeting and the voting procedure to be utilized.

Among the suggestions a mediator can present for consideration by the parties are the following:

1. Affirmative Presentation of Tentative Agreement

The chairman and committee should make an affirmative presentation of the contractual gains, rather than emphasize that which could not be achieved at the bargaining table. All too often, mediators have witnessed equitable settlements rejected because of the inept presentation of the terms before the membership meeting by local officials. It weakens any presentation to remind the members of a bargaining goal which had to be compromised. In a word, there should be an accentuation of the positive.

In drafting or outlining the report to the membership, management representatives can be of material assistance to the union officials charged with this responsibility. Employers often have more sophisticated and extensive communication techniques than those available to most local union leaders. There is no reason why this employer expertise should not be made available to the union leaders for use in "selling" the tentative agreement.

2. Advising Membership of Settlement Terms in Advance of Meeting

There are advantages and disadvantages in informing the union membership in advance of the meeting of the basic terms of the tentative agreement.

The traditional practice has been not to disclose the terms of the settlement prior to the membership meeting. There have been two main reasons for the adoption of this procedure. First it assures the maximum attendance at the membership meeting. People will be motivated to attend because of a quite natural curiosity as to the nature of the new benefits which they will receive under the new contract. A prior disclosure destroys the motivation to attend by those who are in basic agreement with the new contract and brings to the meeting only those who are dissatisfied. Second, non-disclosure prevents political opponents from disparaging the terms of the new agreement and marshalling opposition to it.

In light of the complexity of some settlements, union representatives should perhaps reevaluate the traditional procedure. When settlements include items relating to changes in wage structure, pensions, insurance and health and welfare benefits, it is difficult for the rank and file member to digest the details in an oral presentation.

3. Value of a Quick Meeting Versus a Delayed Meeting

Whether the union should schedule a membership meeting promptly after the tentative agreement or delay doing so is a matter which deserves more careful consideration than is normally given to it.

A quick meeting often has value in that it prevents distorted versions of the tentative agreement from running rampant among the rank and file. All too often, despite a pledge of secrecy, when there is a delay, bits and pieces of the final package leak out and the dissident group can capitalize on the information.

In some cases, however, a quick membership meeting may not be desirable. This is particularly true when the union officers need time properly to organize the material and strategy for the meeting.

4. Stop-Work Versus Off-Premises Meeting

One of the bitterest complaints mediators often hear from union representatives is the lack of attendance at ratification meetings. The apathy of the average union member in union affairs often creates the climate conducive to a domination of the meeting by dissident elements.

The primary object of a union membership meeting, including the ratification meeting, is to assure the maximum attendance and, ideally, participation of a substantial majority of the members. It is only when there is such attendance that the actions taken can truly be said to reflect the desires of the employees in the bargaining unit.

A stop-work meeting is one conducted during the normal work hours on or adjacent to the plant affected. These are normally held at the beginning or end of a shift. The holding of a stop-work ratification meeting has proved to be quite effective in foreclosing the possibility of rejection by a minority since it assures maximum attendance.

The objections to such a meeting are that it disrupts production and may create the impression of company domination of the

93

union. Assuming that the union has operated throughout the contract year as an aggressive representative of the employees, the
latter objection appears to have little validity. While the fact
that a stop-work meeting does interrupt production cannot be
denied, the consideration should be the weighing of the loss of a
few hours against the possibility of a complete shutdown if the
tentative agreement is rejected.

The stop-work meeting in some cases does have the disadvantage in that it may not give the union officials the opportunity
to create the proper climate for acceptance. However, stop-work
meetings are deserving of serious consideration, as is true of
all the suggestions made in this chapter, only if there is a possibility of a rejection.

5. Pre-Vote Meeting

Where there is an organized dissident group, the ratification
meeting may be a stormy one. Those opposed to the tentative
agreement are usually vociferous in highlighting its deficiencies.
Their technique is one of disrpution. They will often shout down
the report of the negotiating committee and effectively block any
attempt to have either a secret ballot or show of hand vote.

Those who would vote to ratify the settlement are often in-
timidated by these tactics. Often those in favor will remain si-
lent or else be carried away by the loudness of the protest, hesi-
tating to oppose it lest they be deemed weaklings. There is a human tendency to demonstrate that one is as "tough" as his fellow
man.

A technique adopted by several unions is to have a reporting
meeting on one day, followed by a secret ballot vote a day or two
later. This has proven to be quite successful in a number of
cases. Under this approach, a membership meeting is called at
which the union negotiating committee presents the terms of the
proposed settlement. The committee gives a detailed explanation
and then the proposal is open for floor discussion. No matter
what the membership's oral reaction is, no vote is taken at this
meeting.

On the following or within a very few days thereafter, a secret ballot vote is conducted to determine acceptance or rejection.

The basic value of this technique is that it provides the opportunity for the dissident group to shout and rant without permitting its outcries to affect the judgment of those who would vote approval of the settlement. It tends to foreclose the possibility of emotions supplanting reasoning and assures that the decision of the membership will be free of the coercive effect of the pressures exerted by the vocal minority.

6. Time and Place of Ratification Meeting

The time and place of the ratification meeting is often quite important in dealing with the problem of rejections.

The probability of an acceptance is enhanced if maximum membership attendance can be achieved.

In our modern society, there is no longer a void in leisure time entertainment. Television, plays, motion pictures, sporting events, family outings and the like are so readily available that the interest in attending union meetings has diminished sharply.

The scheduling of a membership meeting on a pay day or on an extended weekend should be avoided. Similarly, scheduling a meeting for a time which conflicts with a broadcast of a major sporting event cuts down on anticipated attendance.

If meetings are scheduled at such times, the dissidents will attend while those who might have supported the recommendations absent themselves and a rejection which could have been avoided may take place.

The selection of a meeting site also plays a part. If the meeting place is not readily accessible or is too small to accommodate the expected attendance, problems will be created which could discourage maximum attendance.

7. Attendance of Union International Representative

Often, even though the Union International representative has been involved in the negotiations, the demands on his time will induce him to leave the scene once a tentative agreement has been reached.

In some cases, the presence of the International representatives at the membership meeting may be highly desirable.

95

The International representative is at least one step removed from the interplay of local union politics. His economic future is not normally dependent on the goodwill of a particular rank and file local membership. As a consequence, he is able to advocate a position before the membership which would be fraught with political pitfalls if assumed by a local union officer.

Further, the International representative has a much broader exposure to collective bargaining trends and settlements than the local officers. He is in a much better position to counsel and advise the membership and appraise the fairness and comparability of the settlement terms with those achieved in other area or industry negotiations.

If there is a possibility of a rejection, the International representative should be urged to attend the membership meeting so that at least by his physical presence he can support the recommendations of the bargaining committee.

There are, however, some cases where the presence of the International representative at the membership meeting would be a hindrance to ratification. These cases are those in which there is a strong feeling of autonomy on the part of the local. In such cases the local wants to reach its own decisions without any alleged interference by "outsiders." Mediators know of some cases where locals have warned International representatives to stay away from the bargaining table. Indeed, there are cases where the International representative has been told to leave town.

Obviously in these types of cases, the International representative's presence at the meeting would only enhance the chances of a rejection.

8. Type of Vote

Many persons who should have some expertise in the field of collective bargaining have long harbored the notion that ratification meetings and the type of membership vote required are mandated by the provisions of union constitutions. A study conducted by Herbert J. Lahne of the United States Department of Labor has proven that the assumption is unwarranted.[18] The vast majority

18 Lahne, Herbert J., Union Constitutions and Collective Bargaining Procedures.

96

of union constitutions make no specific provision for the type of vote required to approve a tentative agreement. Indeed in most constitutions there is no provision making even the ratification meeting necessary.

On the other hand, despite the absence of constitutional requirements, local unions have adopted practices concerning ratification meetings and types of vote necessary to approve an agreement which has become, because of the passage of time, unwritten law.

While the necessity for conducting a ratification meeting has a bearing on the problem, the type of membership vote has more relevancy.

In most cases, a secret ballot vote is more valuable than a voice or show of hands vote. As mentioned above, a militant organized minority can dominate a meeting by heckling and shouting. Often, unfortunately, the average union member hesitates to give voice to his disapproval of such tactics. As a result, the loudness of the "no" vote offsets the weaker "yes" response. Under such circumstances, a secret ballot vote would be a fairer approach to ascertaining the true desires of the membership.

A few unions traditionally have ratification votes by referendum. A number of other unions are experimenting with this approach as an answer to the rejection problem. Certainly it has the advantage of secrecy. It also provides the member time to evaluate the settlement proposal dispassionately. The disadvantage is the time lag necessary for the mechanics of checking names and addresses against union records, mailing, return of ballots, examination of ballots which may be subject to subsequent challenge and sorting. This time factor is particularly critical in those cases involving multi-plant negotiation and a geographical spread of union members.

Despite these handicaps, if a secret ballot is not possible or desirable, the feasibility of a referendum ballot is worth exploring.

19 MINIMIZING CRISES IN COLLECTIVE BARGAINING

There are several approaches which can be utilized to minimize crises in collective bargaining, even though there are some situations where a crisis is inevitable and cannot be avoided. To cite a few examples--

1. Either an actual or potential political fight in the labor organization representing the employees in a particular plant. Whether it is an actual or potential, the company is often the victim of the by-plays between the "ins" and the "outs." Both are jockeying for political position. Each is seeking to do that which may be momentarily popular since it may be productive of votes, rather than that which may be both responsible and responsive to the issues being negotiated.

2. A corporate merger or consolidation, in which the acquiring company seeks conformity with its industrial relations policies.

3. Cases where an area or industry wage and fringe pattern has been established and the company is not in an economic position to grant similar gains.

4. Insistence by unions on coordinated bargaining in situations where the company resists any form of such bargaining.

While the best time to minimize crises is during the contract term, rather than at the bargaining table at the expiration of the contract, there are several techniques which can be utilized at the bargaining table which may avoid a crisis.

1. Avoid taking an end position prematurely.

There are many issues which are brought out at the bargaining table which at first appear to be insurmountable, but which, as negotiations proceed, can be solved by careful explorations and discussions. Many issues presented do not reflect the true underlying problems which gave rise to the demand. This is particularly true in a seniority area. Professional mediators have often found that a demand for a sweeping change in the entire seniority system was born of several grievances which were left unsettled. Through careful explorations, these grievances can be brought to the surface. By correcting the grievances, the demand often times becomes less formidable. If the negotiator takes an end position prematurely in such situations and others similar to it, a crisis will immediately develop because it leaves the other party only one alternative--consideration of economic action.

2. Forestall the premature adoption of an end position by the other party.

If by the nature of the discussion the other party takes an end position in front of his committee, it is then difficult for him to retreat from it, even though circumstances may warrant a modification of his position. Such avoidances may be obtained by the judicious use of the caucus device or by the temporary abandonment of a line of argument which will lead inevitably to the assumption of an end position by the other party.

3. Complete honesty in negotiations.

During the course of negotiations, experienced negotiators search out possible areas of accommodation, often on the basis of responses to their inquiries across the bargaining table. If a negotiator consciously or unconsciously leads his counterpart into believing that a compromise is possible in a certain area, it is reasonable to assume that such counterpart may structure his entire bargaining strategy around that indication. If it subsequently develops that he was misled, a crisis will be precipitated.

4. Greater use of subcommittees in negotiations.

The final settlement package should be the result of the participation of all the members of the union committee. To the extent that each has a voice in the structuring of the final settlement, there will be the possibility of the settlement being accepted be enhanced. In most negotiations there are a number of issues such as seniority, insurance, inequities, and the like, which lend themselves to a subcommittee approach. In such instances the use of a subcommittee will do much to minimize the possibility of a deadlock and as a consequence a crisis in the bargaining.

5. Attention to resolution of local issues.

Even where the economic package offered equals or exceeds the area or industry pattern, the failure to resolve local issues can precipitate a crisis and lead to an unexpected stoppage. This is especially true where the issues are deemed to be perennial nuisances.

Recently, a multiplant midwestern company offered an economic package which in most respects exceeded settlements achieved by the union in contracts with its major competitors. As a condition of its offer, the company insisted that the union committee withdraw its demands for fixed work schedules and limitations on foremen doing bargaining unit work. The union negotiators agreed and scheduled a ratification meeting supremely confident that securing approval was a mere formality. To their astonishment, the vote was seven to one to reject and a strike occurred. In ferreting out the reason, it was discovered that the two issues dropped had been urged at the three preceding negotiations and withdrawn at the last moment. The employees affected had determined that they would no longer permit the size of the economic package to submerge resolution of these daily aggravations. By marshalling a vocal dissident group around their cause, they succeeded in voting down the agreement.

An in-depth examination and, if merited, a resolution of local issues can avoid a crisis.

6. Avoiding by negotiators of premature announcements of fixed
   bargaining goals.

Just as the premature announcement of a fixed wage goal can
thwart the ability of a union committee to reach a peaceful accommodation of the dispute so too can a similar position taken by a
management committee.

An announcement by management that as a condition of settlement inefficient work practices be eliminated can create a
crisis. Such local practices, particularly if condoned by management over a long period of time, become "sacred cows" to the
employees affected and are emotionally charged. Any precon-
dition seeking to eliminate or curtail them provides a rallying
point for dissident groups. All other union contractual gains are
ignored.

The more sophisticated management bargainers seek to attain
such goals not by announcing prematurely a rigid position but rather
by permitting them to develop during bargaining as mutual problems which should be resolved through negotiations.

7. Insistence on settlement of one issue as a condition precedent.

A premature crisis in bargaining is often created by the insistence of one side or the other on the settlement of one issue
before any meaningful negotiations can take place on the balance
of the issues. While one can appreciate that many negotiators
feel that one issue is of such paramount importance that it must
be resolved before any other issues can be meaningfully discussed,
an obdurate position on this bargaining strategy can only invoke
a similar position on the part of the other party. The adherence
by one party to this position is often dictated by a fear that either
the money offer or other accommodations will submerge or weaken
the issue in the final settlement. Nevertheless, if an agreement
is the goal and not economic action, this position should be abandoned.

As stated before, the best time to minimize crises is during
a contract term. There are a number of suggestions which have
been made during the contract term which can assist the parties
to avoid a crisis at bargaining time. Each of these suggestions
is centered around the central theme--a breakdown in communications between management and its employees. To permit rumors

101

and unsettled grievances to become rampant is to create the atmosphere of mistrust and frustration, which can only lead to strained relationships. Some of the devices which have been used successfully by companies and unions are:

1. <u>Joint explanation of contract language.</u> All too often the negotiators in a collective bargaining contract lose sight of the fact that, while they may know the contents of the contract and its meaning, the actual administration falls into the hands of lower line supervisors and shop stewards. Often no attempt is made to make sure that these fully understand the meaning and application of the contract language. Several companies have very successfully arranged for meetings, separately or jointly, with the shop stewards and foremen. These meetings are usually co-chaired by a union representative and a representative of a labor relations division of the company. At the meeting, the newly negotiated contract is analyzed section by section and jointly explained as to how it would apply to specific shop situations. Questions are solicited so that a complete understanding can be achieved.

   Particularly successful in this area was the program undertaken by the Lockheed Aircraft Company and the Machinists Union. As a result of their program, there was a dramatic drop in the number of grievances since those who were responsible for the day-to-day administration had a clear understanding of how the contract applies in most situations. The investment in time was amply repaid.

2. <u>Interim review of contract terms.</u> The great majority of contracts are for two or more years duration. A number of companies and unions have established a procedure whereby two or three days are set aside in the middle of the contract term for review of problems which may have arisen as a result of the administration of the contract as negotiated. The most successful approaches have been those in which the meeting is attended by high level union and company representatives.

While many practitioners scoffed at the idea of a collective bargaining contract being considered a living document subject to change during the contract term, events have proved that this theory was not so farfetched as it first appeared. When it becomes obvious that some provisions are unworkable and are creating problems for both labor and management, there should be no obstacle to modifying the contract to meet the needs of both parties. It is axiomatic in law that any contract may be modified by mutual consent at any time. This approach does much to dissipate problems which, if allowed to fester, will tend to bring about a crisis at the contract expiration.

3. Joint Study Committees. The issues that confront most negotiators today are highly complex and technical. Each requires a great deal of study and the services of specialists and experts in a particular subject matter must be utilized. I refer to areas such as insurance, pensions, and incentives. There is no reason in the world why the parties who anticipate these issues should not undertake early joint discussions. Each side can set up a subcommittee whose function will not necessarily be to resolve the problems, but at the very least to get agreement on the economic facts and to delineate the issues in dispute. This would do much to eliminate the situation which mediators frequently observe: the parties approach the bargaining table at contract expiration time without a clear understanding of the full implication and cost of the demands raised by the other side.

4. "Early Bird" Bargaining. While most contracts provide 60 days' notice of reopening of a contract, experience has taught that oftentimes this period for discussion and negotiation is too short. All too often, because of prior commitments of the parties, negotiations are delayed so that the actual negotiation time is cut down substantially. A number of companies and unions recognizing this fact have engaged in what has

been termed "early bird" bargaining. Despite contract provisions calling for a 60-day notice, such parties have started negotiations much in advance of that time. This permitted them to explore in depth various issues and leave ample time for study and possible accommodation. More and more practitioners have adopted this policy of early bargaining and have found it to be, in a number of cases, highly successful. In some cases, it has even resulted in the effectuation of the new wage increase prior to the expiration of the old contract.

5. <u>Job Security Changes.</u> The experience of mediators indicates that one of the greatest causes of stoppages is the fear, real or fancied, of loss of job security. Statistics indicate that when the issue of job security exists, the possibility of a stoppage and a prolonged one, is ever present. If a company is contemplating any changes that have an effect on the job security of its employees, is it not the better part of wisdom for such a company to discuss the contemplated changes with the union representative, much in advance of the institution of such changes?

Fears of loss of job security may arise as a result of automation, mechanization, changes in the seniority practices, consolidation of departments, removal of certain operations from the plant or subcontracting. Normally, the decision of the company to undertake such programs is not one reached at the spur of the moment. A great deal of corporate planning and thought usually goes into it. The inevitable leaks as to what the company is contemplating creates an instability in the employees' outlook even though oftentimes the leaks result in a distorted or exaggerated fear. It is just common sense for any company, when contemplating such a drastic change to sit down with the union representatives and advise them of its plans, seeking their suggestions as to the best manner of implementation which would result in the least dislocation. Fears can thus be quieted and crises at the bargaining table avoided.

6. <u>Telling Company's Story.</u> If the company is facing a marketing and/or tight financial position it should not await bargaining time to try to tell a story to the employees. At bargaining time, the emotions are too high and there will not be a great deal of receptivity to or sympathy for the company's plight.

   In speaking of telling the company story, it is strongly urged that the use of elaborate statistics be avoided. A much more effective way of telling the company's story is to do so in narrative form accompanied by simple charts or graphs.

20 MEDIATION IN THE PUBLIC SECTOR

Federal Mediation and Conciliation Service Involvement in Federal Sector Bargaining Impasses

There is an ever-escalating interest in mediation as at least one of the steps in the resolution of disputes in public sector.

The involvement of the Federal Mediation Service in such disputes was given impetus by the promulgation of Executive Order 10988 which was issued in January 1962.[19]

The main thrust of the Order was to state clearly the government's recognition of federal employees right to form, join and assist any employee organization and to bargain collectively with agencies of government. It established certain criteria and procedures for types of recognition to be accorded to such organizations and outlined the permissive and non-permissive subject matter of bargaining.

Even though it would appear that such an order would encourage the use of established machinery for the resolution of impasses in this sector, the official view was to the contrary.

The Civil Service Commission expressed the official view in Bulletin No. 700-5 issued in April 1962. It emphasized that the Executive Order did not assign any responsibility to the Federal Service to give labor relations advice to other agencies or departments nor did it authorize that Service to make its mediation facilities available in collective bargaining disputes in the federal sector.

It should be noted that while the bulletin did not authorize the extension of mediation services to such disputes nevertheless

---

[19] See Appendix I

it did not prohibit it. It did, however, effectively end for the next two or three years serious requests for Federal Mediation and Conciliation Service involvement in such collective bargaining disputes.

slowed by leg.

Starting with 1965, because of the spectacular growth in the unionization of federal and state employees, the hiatus ended. Union representatives and agency managers were again requesting not only labor relations advice but also mediation assistance from the Federal Mediation and Conciliation Service.

speed up

In light of these developments, the Service began a reevaluation and reassessment of its 1962 position. Even though the mediation process has its limitations, it was clear that it could materially assist in the resolution of many of the impasses which were occurring. The Service initiated a series of meetings with the Civil Service Commission, and other appropriate agencies and departments. It also conferred with representatives of labor organizations representing federal employees. As a result of these meetings and its own experience, on February 7, 1966, the Civil Service Commission officially advised all federal agencies of its new policy. Its communication stated in part:

> "Among the techniques mentioned, mediation is probably the most appropriate method for dealing with important and difficult issues that remain unsolved after earnest efforts by the parties to reach agreement through direct negotiations."

With this endorsement behind it, the Service established an unpublicized policy and procedure for the consideration of mediation requests in the Federal Service. It was the opinion of the Service that it could offer assistance only on a very limited and selective basis. There were a number of factors which dictated this course of action--an overloaded staff, a limited budget and a caution about entering a field which because of the lack of a deadline could unduly prolong mediation involvement.

The internal policy adopted provided:

1. All requests for mediation had to be screened and decided at the National Office level in Washington, D.C.

107

2. No request would be considered unless made jointly by both parties and usually in writing.

3. No request would be considered unless both parties certified an impasse had been reached following genuine bargaining efforts.

4. In the event a joint request was approved, the Service would select and assign the individual mediator.

5. The mediator assigned would be available only for a limited period of time and/or a limited number of joint meetings as the situation dictated.

Within the limitations of the foregoing policy, the Service entered into a period of experimentation. In the federal sector, its mediation services were utilized by a number of Government agencies and unions including Tennessee Valley Authority, Bureau of Mines, Army, Navy and Air Force. The issues presented dealt with the distribution and assignment of overtime; recall and lay-off procedures; apprenticeship programs and training; paid time for authorized union business; disciplinary actions; sick and annual leave; parking problems; job descriptions and the like.

Three federal agencies wrote into their agreements provisions requesting the services of the Federal Mediation and Conciliation Service in impasse situations--the Post Office, Labor and Navy Departments.

It was found that in the main, the techniques its mediators developed in the private sector were relevant and applicable to the public sector. In all but one of the cases in which the Service exercised jurisdiction, the parties were able to reach agreement with the assistance of the assigned mediator.

While the Executive Order 10988 did establish a federal policy relating to the duty of the various governmental agencies to recognize and bargain with representatives of their employees, it soon proved to need updating in light of the experience under the Order and the meteoric rise of organization among federal employees.

To accomplish this end, the President established the President's Review Committee on Federal Employee-Management Relations. The Committee held many meetings to solicit the viewpoints of the agencies, union organizations and other interested parties.

As a result of its investigation, the Committee concluded that there were six areas which required changes in Executive Order 10988. Among the six was the following:

"Third party processes for resolving disputes on unit and election questions, for investigation and resolution of complaints...and for assistance in resolving negotiation impasse problems and grievances."

In the area of resolution of negotiation impasse problems, the Committee recommended:

"(1) The Federal Mediation and Conciliation Service should extend its services to the Federal labor relations program.

"(2) A Federal Service Impasse Panel should be established to assist the parties if they are unable to reach agreement through other available means. The panel should be authorized to provide fact finding on the issues and make recommendations to the parties as a basis for settlement. In the event all issues are not settled within 30 days, the panel should have authority to take whatever action it deems necessary to bring the dispute to a settlement."

Further, the Committee echoed the thoughts of the task force which preceded Executive Order 10988 about the inhibiting effect on negotiations of a ready availability of third party procedures for the resolution of negotiation impasses.

In speaking of the Federal Mediation and Conciliation Service, the Committee stated:

"In recent years, the Federal Mediation and Conciliation Service has provided mediation services to the Federal program on a limited, experimental basis. The success of its efforts has amply demonstrated that use of the Service's facilities in the Federal labor-management relations program should be expanded to the maximum extent practicable. To this end, we recommend that the Federal Mediation and Conciliation Service be authorized to extend full services to the Federal program, subject to such necessary rules as it may prescribe. It should provide the same type of mediation assistance that it offers in the private sector, without charge to either party, including preventive mediation services. The parties to an impasse should, of course, continue on a cost-sharing basis by persons of their choice other than Federal Mediation and Conciliation Service commissioners.

"We believe, further, that at this stage of the Federal program additional governmental assistance should be made available when earnest efforts by the parties to reach agreement through direct negotiations, referral to higher authority within the department or agency and the national office of the labor organizations, and the services of the Federal Mediation and Conciliation Service or other third-party mediation have been unavailing in bringing the parties to the point of full agreement."

Pursuant to the Committee's recommendations, in October 1969, an Executive Order 11491[20] was issued entitled "Labor-Management Relations in the Federal Service."

A Federal Service Impasse Panel was established to deal with negotiation disputes and impasses. The Order charged the Federal Mediation and Conciliation Service to provide mediation assistance to Federal agencies and labor organizations.

---

[20] See Appendix J

It further provided that when "voluntary arrangements, including the services of the Federal Mediation and Conciliation Service or other third party mediation failed to resolve the dispute," the Impasse Panel could assume jurisdiction.

In October 1970, the Impasse Panel issued its rules and published them in the Federal Register.[21]

Section 2471.1 of those rules provides that in the event of an impasse in negotiations, the Panel's consideration can be invoked (a) by either party, (b) by both parties jointly, (c) by the Federal Mediation and Conciliation Service, or (d) the Panel can intervene on its own motion.

This section appears to disregard the clear caution expressed by the Presidential Review Committee. The Committee, in agreeing with the 1961 Presidential task force, warned that the ready availability of third party procedures could cause an undesired escalation effect.

History has taught that whenever another forum, over and beyond collective bargaining and mediation, is made readily available to negotiators, it inhibits collective bargaining. Access to another forum often gives negotiators a reason to avoid making the hard decisions necessary to reach an accommodation during collective bargaining. Under these circumstances, many union and company negotiators are reulctant to recede from prior positions if there is a possibility that the dispute may be resolved by another agency with greater powers than mediation.

The rules of the Impasse Panel invite recourse to it and may have the escalating effect which both Presidential committees warned against. In the words of the Review Committee..."the parties, instead of working out their differences by hard, earnest and serious negotiation, (will) continually take their problems to a third party for settlement."

The better procedure would appear to be to provide that the Impasse Panel would not assume jurisdiction unless and until the Federal Mediation Service had certified to it that an impasse has been reached in the negotiations, despite the efforts of the parties and of the Service, and that a resolution of the dispute does not appear possible in the foreseeable future. This is essentially the same procedure as was followed by the War Labor Board during World War II.

---

21 See Appendix K

Further, the Presidential committee made it quite clear that the Impasse Panel should be made available "when earnest efforts by the parties...and the services of the Federal Mediation and Conciliation Service of other third party mediation have been unavailing...." It is hard to reconcile the recommendations of the Committee with the Impasse Panel's rules providing for access to the Panel without prior recourse to the mediation process.

It is also difficult to understand a position assumed by the Presidential Committee and the Impasse Panel in requiring prior approval of the Panel before the parties voluntarily can resort to fact-finding or arbitration. The Committee in its recommendation stated:

> "it (Federal Mediation and Conciliation Service) should provide that same type of mediation assistance that it offers in the private sector...."

In the private sector, the Mediation Service provides arbitration service and is admonished in Section 302(c) of the Labor-Management Relations Act to..."seek to induce the parties volunatrily to seek other means of settling the dispute...."

"Other means" encompasses arbitration and fact-finding and its equivalent--advisory arbitration. Quite often, particularly on the eve of the contract expiration, if a stoppage appears inevitable, the mediator will urge the parties to submit the issues in dispute to either arbitration or fact-finding.

Further, one of the basic tools utilized by mediators, in appropriate cases in the private sector, is a formal recommendation as a basis for the resolution of the dispute. Under the Executive Order and the rules of the Impasse Panel, the mediator is deprived of even this tool.

Both the Presidential Committee and the Impasse Panel have deprived the mediator of several of the alternatives which may be utilized to avoid a stoppage.

Mediation Techniques Utilized in the Public Sector

While the basic tools of mediation are applicable to most disputes in the public sector, there are essential factors characteristic of public sector disputes which call for additional mediation procedures.

One of the major inducements to the parties in the private sector to reach agreement is the possibility of a strike or lockout. This pressure point is missing in the public sector because of either an outright ban or a curtailment on the right to engage in a strike.

In the public sector, the mandatory subject matters of bargaining are limited. These limitations flow from structural differences between the two areas. The ability to provide benefits and improve working conditions in the public sector does not stem from a free enterprise or profit system but almost totally from the tax or regulatory structure which is essentially political in nature.

Another characteristic of the public sector which calls for a different mediation approach is the lack of collective bargaining expertise on the part of most representatives of the parties. To most, collective bargaining is a new experience. Many representatives, whose education, training and experience are far divorced from the training and experience required at the bargaining table, find themselves propelled into a field completely foreign to them.

Closely allied to this lack of expertise, is the tendency on the part of the representatives of both parties in the public sector to seek third party assistance in the solution of their problems. Often they prefer an imposed or endorsed settlement so that the responsibility and onus of decision making is shifted away from themselves. In that way they can escape the ire of their superiors or their constituency.

Another difficulty a mediator encounters in the public sector is the lack of authority granted to the agency's representatives. It is the hope that the new Executive Order will encourage agencies to delegate more authority to officials at the bargaining unit level.

Finally, because of the high visibility of most disputes in the public sector, negotiators and the mediator find themselves bargaining in a fish bowl. Such type of bargaining hampers the "hair down" give-and-take of normal negotiations which is so essential to reaching an agreement in the private sector.

To accommodate to these difficulties, a mediator must innovate new techniques over and beyond the techniques he utilizes in the private sector.

One of the techniques found to be effective is the creation of an artificial deadline.

In one public sector dispute, the parties had been negotiating from some 15 months without concluding an agreement. The services of a mediator were then requested. After three days on the secne, the mediator announced he was withdrawing if agreement was not consummated by the end of the sixth day. On the fifth day, an agreement was concluded.

In another public sector case, negotiations had been conducted on a desultory basis for some ten or eleven months. When a mediator was requested the appointing agency advised both parties that because of the mediator's prior commitments he could only be available for seven bargaining sessions. An agreement was reached at the fifth bargaining session.

This device has been used by mediators in several other cases and with a degree of success. The establishment of an artificial deadline brought to the bargaining table a sense of urgency which motivated the negotiators to make the hard decisions which were necessary to effect an accommodation.

Because of the paucity of expertise on the part of the representatives of the parties and the consequent lack of confidence on their part as to the degree of authority reposed in them, there is a tendency to look to the third party neutral to take the onus of suggesting a solution to the issue or issues in dispute. As a result, mediators in the public sector often resort to making informal recommendations to the parties as to the possible compromise or solution of the dispute. Such recommendations of course are not binding on the parties. In the private sector, a mediator will normally avoid making recommendations unless the dispute meets the criteria set forth in Chapter .

Finally, in the private sector, mediators will seldom appeal from the position taken by the bargaining table negotiator to his superiors. Mediators realize the need to maintain and respect the status of the negotiator no matter how unreasonable his position on an issue may appear to be. To bypass such negotiator may jeopardize not only the mediator's acceptability and effectiveness in the future but also endanger the future collective bargaining relations between the parties.

In the public sector, a mediator in many cases will not hesitate to appeal to higher authority especially if he is persuaded that the position of the bargainer stems from lack of delegated authority. Indeed in a number of cases agency representatives welcome or invite the actions of the mediator.

The public sector field is comparatively new. Undoubtedly as mediators gain additional insights into the bargaining limitations imposed on negotiators they will innovate to meet the new challenge.

21 PRICING WAGE AND FRINGE OFFERS AND DEMANDS

It is often helpful, in the course of both mediation and negotiation efforts, for one party or the other to direct attention to the cost impact of a particular offer or demand.

All too often the parties will become so engrossed in their argumentation that they lose their perspective insofar as the financial burdens,a concession or demand would have on the company involved.

Since economic demands are couched in terms of cents per hour or one additional holiday, the parties, and especially the union committee, may very well feel that the difference between their respective positions is infinitesimal and chide the other side with being niggardly in their adamantcy. It is quite easy for the union to point out that the difference between their demands and the company's position is only 2¢ or 3¢ which on the face seems trite. However, if the difference is translated into dollar impact on annual payroll, an entirely different picture may be painted. The "trite" difference may impose on the company a $50,000 to $100,000 increase on its annual labor bill.

1. General Wage Increase Offers or Demands

a. Impact on annual payroll costs.

The direct impact of a general wage increase on annual payroll costs can be readily computed.

Assume that there are 5,000 employees in the bargaining unit and the wage offer is 6¢ per hour. To determine the direct impact on annual payroll costs, the computation would be:

1¢ increase per hour per employee per year =
(40 hours x 52 weeks x 1¢) = $20.80
2080 hours x 6¢ offered = $124.00 per employee
per year.
$124.00 x 5,000 employees = $620,000 total annual additional payroll cost.

Sometimes the base used is the scheduled work year or
total productive time which can be either 2,000 or 2,040
hours.

It should be emphasized that this figure represents only
the direct impact. To this must be added the indirect impact a wage increase would have on incentives, premium
pay, shift differentials, overtime, holiday and vacation pay,
severance pay, pensions, and other benefits.

b. Average cost of general increases for contract of two or
more years' duration.

The total cost of a general increase can be computed either as (a) total cost, or (b) average cost during the term
of the contract.

A contract of three years' duration providing for annual
increases of 30¢ the first year, 25¢ the second year and 20¢
the third year, entails a total cost of 75¢ per hour per employee.

To compute the average cost:

Cents		Years		
30	x	3	=	90
25	x	2	=	50
20	x	1	=	20
				160

3 years ÷ 160 = 53 1/3¢ average cost per hour per
employee.

c. Computing cost of night shift premium.

To determine the cost of a night shift premium or an in-crease in an established night shift premium, multiply the percentage of employees affected by the night shift premium or increase in such premium.

Illustration

Assume a plant employing 400 workers of which 50 are on the night shift.   To determine the cost of a 15¢ an hour shift premium:

$$\frac{50}{400} = .125$$

$$.125 \times .15 = \$.01875$$

Fringe Cost Computations

No attempt is made here to reach conclusions as to por-tion of the total wage dollar spent for fringe benefits. Most of such studies are meaningless unless the surveyor enu-merates the exact items he has designated "fringes" for the purpose of his report. The term "fringes" escapes precise definition. The resultant cost figure will expand or contract in direct relationship to the broadness or narrowness of the description of "fringes" used.

To assist mediators and negotiators, we will treat only some of the more commonly accepted fringes. For collec-tive bargaining purposes, fringe offers and demands can be expressed in terms of (a) total annual cost to the company, or (b) cents per hour per employee.

d. Cents per hour costs.

The determination of costs in terms of cents per hour presents some difficulties in that the results may differ de-pending on the basic formula used. There are four basic formulas--each valid--which have been used.

1.   Cents per straight time productive hours. The productive hours would be the straight time hours minus paid time off.

2.   Cents per straight time hours.   The straight time hours would be based on the scheduled work year, e. g., 2,040 hours.

3.   Determining cents cost by dividing the annual cost of the fringe by the total productive man-hours.   Productive man-hours can be determined by adding straight time hours and overtime hours and deducting paid time off.

4.   Cents per straight time hour based on an arbitrary figure for annual work.

The use of these basic formulae will yield the cents per hour cost of other fringes such as vacations, rest periods, wash-up time and the like.

e.   Computing cost of holidays.

1.   Total annual cost.   If a contract provides for eight paid holidays and the plant employs 500 workers in the bargaining unit with an average hourly rate of $3.00--the total cost of the holidays can be computed by the following formula:

Number of workers X average hourly rate X hours off on holidays.

Applying the formula to the example cited:

500 employees X 3.00 X 64 hours = $96,000 annual cost.

2.   Cost in cents per hour.   The following formula would be applicable:

Annual Cost ÷ Average Hours Worked per Year X Number of Employees.

Applying this formula to the above example:

119

$$\frac{96,000}{2080 \times 500} = 9.33¢ \text{ per hour}$$

3. **Total annual cost per employee.** To determine total annual cost per employee:

$$\frac{\text{Company Annual Cost}}{\text{Total Number of Employees}}$$

$$\frac{96,000}{500} = \$192.00$$

f. Computing cost of vacations.

In computing cost of vacations, one must take into account the seniority of employees and their eligibility for vacations based on such seniority.

Let us assume that a contract calls for one week of vacation after one year of service, two weeks after three years of service, three weeks after ten years of service, and four weeks after twenty years of service. Let us use as an illustration a 500-man plant with average hourly earnings of $3.00. One hundred employees have one year seniority; 300 have more than 3 years, but less than 10; 70 have 10 years, but less than 20; and 30 have 20 or more years of service. The following would be an application of the formula:

$$
\begin{array}{rcr}
100 \times 40 \times \$3.00 & = & \$12,000 \\
300 \times 80 \quad\;\; 3.00 & = & 72,000 \\
70 \times 120 \times 3.00 & = & 25,200 \\
30 \times 160 \times 3.00 & = & \underline{14,400} \\
\text{Total annual cost} \ldots\ldots & & \$123,600
\end{array}
$$

g. Computing costs of wash-up time or rest periods.

To compute the cost of wash-up time or rest periods, the following formula may be utilized:

120

$$\frac{\text{Time Off Per Day}}{60} \times \text{Average Hourly Rate} \div \text{num-}$$

ber of hours in workday of employees who would receive the off time.

To illustrate: if two rest periods of 10 minutes each are granted to 100 employees in a plant where the average rate is $3.00 an hour and the normal workday is 8 hours:

$\frac{20 \text{ minutes}}{60 \text{ minutes}} = .33$ (portion of one hour represented by rest period time)

3.00 x .33 = $1.00   (cost per day per employee)

$\frac{\$1.00}{8 \text{ hrs.}} = .125$ or 12 1/2¢ (cost per hour per employee)

If the number of employees who receive the rest period or wash-up time is less than the total number of employees in the bargaining unit to which the cost calculation applies, multiply cost per hour per employee by the percent of employees who will receive the fringe benefit.

2. Pension Plans

Costing an existing or newly negotiated pension plan depends on a number of factors and assumptions.

Unless certain basic information is made available, proper costing becomes impossible. Information that is required for each individual in the group to be covered relates to:

1. Age
2. Seniority
3. Sex
4. Rate of pay (if plan is to be salary related)

In addition some agreement must be reached as to the assumptions to be utilized in arriving at a cost figure such as the rate of return on investment, period and method of funding and the like.

121

As a general guide, the operating costs of a pension plan can be determined by the use of the following formula:

Costs = Benefits Less Investment Earnings Plus
Administration Expenses.

Past service liability is determined by estimating the present value of all benefits at the present or current age of each employee and subtracting the present value of future normal contributions.

The following table prepared by the AFL-CIO (published in its excellent work entitled "Pension Plans Under Collective Bargaining") can be of assistance to the practitioner to determine the approximate cost per year per employee for a pension plan with values varying with the average age and average seniority of the group. Caution must be used in using the table since costs also vary in relationship to the distribution of the group by age and seniority.

Further the table makes the following assumptions:

a. Rate of return - 3 3/4%
b. Mortality Tables of 1949
c. Vesting after 10 years
d. Retirement at age 65
e. Typical seniority distribution
f. All male work force
g. Normal administration costs
h. Past service liability over a 25-year period.

3. Costing the Insurance Package

While the cost of an insurance program is dependent on experience, sex and age mix, and other similar factors, it is often useful for the bargaining table representative to be able to gauge quickly an approximation of the cost impact of a demand or offer.

The following are suggested general "rules of thumb" which may be helpful until there is an opportunity to gather data for a more accurate costing.

Approximate Cost of Pension of $1.00 per Month per Year of Service Depending Upon Average Age & Average Years of Service
(In Dollars per Year per Employee)

Years of Service	Average Age 27	28	29	30	31	32	33	34	35	36	37	38	39	40	41	42	43	44	45	46	47	48	49	50
0	40	42	44	46	48	50	52	54	56	58	60	62	62	64										
1	42	44	46	48	50	52	54	56	58	60	62	64	64	66	68									
2	44	46	48	50	52	54	56	58	60	62	64	68	68	70	72	76								
3	46	48	50	52	54	56	58	60	62	64	66	70	70	72	74	80	84							
4	48	50	52	54	56	58	60	62	64	68	70	72	74	76	78	82	86	88						
5	50	52	54	56	58	60	62	64	68	70	72	74	76	78	80	86	88	92						
6		54	56	58	62	62	66	66	70	72	74	76	80	82	84	90	92	94	94	96	100	104	106	110
7			60	62	64	64	68	70	72	74	78	80	82	84	86	92	96	98	96	100	104	108	110	114
8				64	68	68	70	72	74	76	80	82	86	88	90	96	98	102	100	104	108	110	114	118
9					70	72	74	76	78	80	82	86	88	92	92	100	102	106	104	108	112	114	118	122
10						74	76	78	80	82	86	90	92	94	96	102	104	108	108	112	114	118	122	126
11							78	80	82	84	88	92	94	96	98	106	108	112	112	114	116	122	126	130
12								82	84	86	90	94	96	98	102	108	110	114	114	118	120	124	128	132
13									86	90	92	96	98	102	104	110	114	116	118	120	124	128	132	136
14										92	94	98	100	104	108	112	116	118	120	122	128	132	136	140
15											96	100	102	106	110	114	118	122	122	126	132	136	140	144
16												102	104	108	112	116	122	124	126	128	136	140	144	148
17													106	110	114	118	124	128	128	132	140	142	145	152
18														112	116	120	126	130	132	134	142	144	148	154
19															118	122	128	132	134	138	144	148	152	158
20																124	128	132	136	140	146	150	156	162

Source: AFL-CIO, Pension Plans Under Collective Bargaining

1. Life Insurance
   70¢ per month per employee for each $1,000.

2. Sickness and Accident
   70¢ per month for each $10 for 26 weeks.

3. Hospitalization
   (including full cost of miscellaneous charges)
   17¢ per dollar for employees alone.
   42¢ per dollar for dependents.

4. Surgical ($300 schedule with $100 maternity)

5. Doctor in Hospital ($5 a day for 70 days)
   17¢ a month for employee.
   26¢ a month for dependents.

6. Polio ($1500 coverage)
   2¢ a month for employee.
   5¢ a month for family.

7. Doctor
   (in hospital, home and office--$5-$3-$3 schedule)
   69¢ a month for employee.
   $2.50 a month for family.

8. Major Medical ($100 deductible--80-20 coinsurance)
   $1.00 a month for employee.
   $2.00 a month for family.

9. Accidental Death and Dismemberment
   8¢ to 10¢ per month per thousand.

Bibliography

BIBLIOGRAPHY

"Impartial Opinion and Constructive Criticism of Mediators, Mediation Agencies and Conciliators"
>   ANGOFF, Samuel E.
>>   Address to Association of State Mediation Agencies at Ninth Annual Conference, 1960, Connecticut
>>   (Labor Law Journal, January 1961, pp. 67-72)

"The Mediation Process"
>   BULLEN, Frederick H.
>>   New York University, First Annual Conference, 1948, pp. 105-143

"The State Mediator: Background, Self-Image, and Attitudes"
>   BERKOWITZ, Monroe
>   GOLDSTEIN, Bernard
>   INDIK, Bernard
>>   Industrial and Labor Relations Review, January 1964, Vol. 17, pp. 257-275

"The Mediation Process"
>   WARREN, Edgar L. and BERNSTEIN, Irving
>>   Southern Economic Journal, April 1949, Vol. 15, pp. 441-457

"Selecting Supervisory Mediators through Trial by Combat"
>   GELLHORN, Walter and BRODY, William
>>   Public Administration Review, November 1948, pp. 259-266

"The Conciliation Process"
    CHALMERS, Ellison W.
        Industrial and Labor Relations Review, April 1948,
        pp. 337-350

Industrial Peacemaking--A Report on Union-Management
Negotiations
    DOUGLAS, Ann
        New York, Columbia University Press, 1962

"What Can Research Tell Us About Mediation?"
    DOUGLAS, Ann
        Labor Law Journal, August 1955, pp. 545-552

✓ "Federal Mediation: How It Works"
    FINNEGAN, Joseph F.
        Depaul Law Review, Autumn-Winter 1959, Vol. 9, pp. 1-8

The Mediator
    INDIK, Bernard P.
        Research Program, Institute of Management and Labor
        Relations, Rutgers University

Meeting of Minds: A Way to Peace Through Mediation
    JACKSON, Elmore
        McGraw-Hill Book Company, Inc., 1952
        pp. 24-38, pp. 119-164

"The United States Federal Mediation and Conciliation Service:
Catalyst to Collective Bargaining"
    KELTNER, John W.
        International Labour Review, Vol. 88, No. 5, pp. 3-16

"Industrial Conflict and Its Mediation"
    KERR, Clark
        American Journal of Sociology, Vol. 60, November 1954,
        pp. 230-245

"Mediation and the Psychology of Small Groups"
    KNOWLES, William J.
        Labor Law Journal, October 1958, pp. 780-784

"The Behavior and Personality of the Labor Mediator:
The Parties' Perception of Mediator Behavior"
(Interim Report of a Research Project in Mediation)
    LANDSBERGER, Henry A.
        Labor Law Journal, August 1955, pp. 552-560

"The Behavior and Personality of the Labor Mediator:
The Parties' Perception of Mediator Behavior"
    LANDSBERGER, Henry A.
        Personnel Psychology, Vol. 13, No. 3, Autumn 1960,
        pp. 329-347

"Final Report on a Research Project in Mediation"
    LANDSBERGER, Henry A.
        Labor Law Journal, August 1956, pp. 501-508

"The Mediation Process"
    LOVELL, Hugh G.
        Thesis paper submitted in partial fulfillment of the re-
        quirements for the degree of Doctor of Philosophy, Mas-
        sachusetts Institute of Technology, 1951, 51 pages.

"The Pressure Lever in Mediation"
    LOVELL, Hugh G.
        Industrial and Labor Relations Review, October 1952,
        pp. 20-30

"Mediators and Their Qualifications"
    MANSON, Julius J.
        Labor Law Journal, October 1958, pp. 755-764

Fact Finding in Public Employment Disputes--Promise or Illusion
    McKELVEY, Jean Trepp
        1968 Winter Proceedings, Industrial Relations Research
        Association

"Grievance Mediation under Collective Bargaining"
McPHERSON, William H.
Industrial and Labor Relations Review, January 1956,
pp. 200-212

"Drawing Jurisdictional Lines in Mediation"
MEAD, John F. and KRISLOV, Joseph
Monthly Labor Review, April 1969

"Function of the Mediator in Collective Bargaining"
MEYER, Arthur S.
Industrial and Labor Relations Review, Vol. 13
January 1960, pp. 159-165

"Mediation of Public Employee Disputes"
MOSKOWITZ, George, CHISHOLM, Allen D.
Labor Law Journal, January 1961, pp. 53-61

"Mediation--The Viewpoint of the Mediated"
NORTHRUP, Herbert R.
Labor Law Journal, October 1962, pp. 832-840
Address to the Association of State Mediation Agencies at
their Eleventh Annual Conference, 1962, Quebec, Canada

"Psychological Factors in Industrial Mediation"
PASTER, Irving
Personnel, September 1954, pp. 15-127

"Evaluation of Mediation Techniques"
PEREZ, Francisco Aponte
Labor Law Journal, October 1959, pp. 716-720

Conciliation in Action--Principles and Techniques
PETERS, Edward
National Foremen's Institute, Inc.
New London, Connecticut (1952)

Strategy and Tactics in Labor Negotiations
PETERS, Edward
National Foremen's Institute, Inc.
New London, Connecticut (1955)

"Preventive Mediation--A Technique to Improve
Industrial Relations"
PRASOW, Paul
Labor Law Journal, August 1950, pp. 866-868

"Mediation of Industrial Conflict"
REHMUS, Charles M.
9 Journal of Conflict Resolution 1

"Needed Research in the Mediation of Labor Disputes"
ROSE, Arnold
Personnel Psychology, 1952, Vol. 5, pp. 187-200

"Code of Professional Conduct for Labor Mediators"
SIMKIN, William E.
Labor Law Journal, October 1964, Vol. 15, pp. 627-631

"Are There Too Many Mediators"
STARK, Arthur
Labor Law Journal, January 1955, pp. 33-41

"An Analysis of the Activities of the Federal Mediation
and Conciliation Service in the Metropolitan Area of
Birmingham, Alabama"
STEEN, Jack E.
Thesis paper submitted in partial fulfillment of the re-
quirements for the degree of Doctor of Philosophy, School
of Commerce and Business Administration, University of
Alabama, 1965, 219 pages.

"Mediation Function and Tactics"
STEVENS, Carl M.
Strategy and Collective Bargaining Negotiations
(McGraw-Hill, 1963, pp. 123-146)

"Troikas, Duets, and Prima Donnas in Labor Mediation"
STUTZ, Robert L.
Labor Law Journal, October 1962, pp. 845-851

"Management in Mediation--A Mediator's View"
    VALTIN, Rolf
        Personnel, September 1956, Vol. 33, pp. 118-129

"Mediation and Fact Finding"
    WARREN, Edgar L.
        Industrial Conflict, Chapter 22, pp. 292-300
        (McGraw-Hill Book Co., Inc., 1954)

"Some Thoughts on Labor Mediation"
    WEISENFELD, Allan
        Industrial Relations Research Association,
        December 1953, pp. 276-283

Mediation and the Development of Industrial Relations
in New Jersey
    WEISENFELD, Allan
    New Jersey State Board of Mediation

"Profile of a Labor Mediator"
    WEISENFELD, Allan
        Labor Law Journal, October 1962, pp. 864-873
        (Paper delivered to the Association of State Mediation
        Agencies at their Eleventh Annual Conference, 1962,
        Quebec, Canada)

"The Personal Factor in Labor Mediation"
    WESCHLER, Irving R.
        Personnel Psychology, Summer 1950, Vol. 3, pp. 113-132
        Personnel, November 1949, Vol. 26, pp. 222-226

" 'Communications' and Mediation"
    YAGER, Paul
        Labor Law Journal, August 1953, pp. 539-540

"Mediation as a Harmonizing Influence in Collective Bargaining"
    YOUNG, Stanley
        Personnel Administration, September 1959, pp. 21-287

130

Appendices

Appendix A

FEDERAL MEDIATION AND CONCILIATION
SERVICE: ARBITRATION POLICIES,
FUNCTIONS, AND PROCEDURES

Chapter XII--Federal Mediation and
Conciliation Service

PART 1404--ARBITRATION

On June 21, 1968, notice of proposed rule changes was published in the FEDERAL REGISTER (68 F.R. 7358). There were set out therein the proposed revisions of Chapter XII, Title 29, of the Code of Federal Regulations, relating to the Service's arbitration policies and procedures. Comments which were received concerning the proposed regulations have been considered. The amendatory regulations as set forth below are hereby adopted to be effective October 21, 1968, and shall as of that date supersede the present regulations which are set forth in 29 CFR Part 1404.

Sec.

1404.1	Arbitration.
1404.2	Composition of roster maintained by the Service.
1404.3	Security Status.
1404.4	Procedures; how to request arbitration services.
1404.5	Arbitrability.
1404.6	Nominations of arbitrators.
1404.7	Appointment of arbitrators.
1404.8	Status of arbitrators after appointment.
1404.9	Prompt decision.
1404.10	Arbitrator's award and report.
1404.11	Fees of arbitrators.
1404.12	Conduct of hearings.

AUTHORITY: The provisions of this Part 1404 issued under sec. 202, 61 Stat. 153, as amended; 29 U.S.C. 172. Interpret or apply sec. 3, 80 Stat. 250, sec. 203, 61 Stat. 153; 5 U.S.C. 552, 29 U.S.C. 173.

1404.1 Arbitration.

The labor policy of the U. S. Government is designed to foster and promote free collective bargaining. Voluntary arbitration is encouraged by public policy and is in fact almost universally utilized by the parties to resolve disputes involving the interpretation or application of collective bargaining agreements. Also, in appropriate cases, voluntary arbitration or factfinding are tools of free collective bargaining and may be desirable alternatives to economic strife in determining terms of a collective bargaining agreement. The parties assume broad responsibilities for the success of the private juridical system they have chosen. The Service will assist the parties in their selection of arbitrators.

1404.2 Composition of roster maintained by the Service.

(a) It is the policy of the Service to maintain on its roster only those arbitrators who are qualified and acceptable, and who adhere to ethical standards.

(b) Applicants for inclusion on its roster must not only be well-grounded in the field of labor-management relations, but, also, usually possess experience in the labor arbitration field or its equivalent. After a careful screening and evaluation of the applicant's experience, the Service contacts representatives of both labor and management since arbitrators must be generally acceptable to those who utilize its arbitration facilities. The responses to such inquiries are carefully weighed before an otherwise qualified arbitrator is included on the Service's roster. Persons employed full time as representatives of management, labor, or of the Federal Government are not included on the Service's roster.

(c) The arbitrators on the roster are expected to keep the Service informed of changes in address, occupation or availability, and of any business connections with or of concern to labor or management. The Service reserves the right to remove names from the active roster or to take other appropriate action where there is good reason to believe that an arbitrator is not adhering to these regulations and related policy.

1404.3 Security status.

The arbitrators on the Service's roster are not employees of the Federal Government, and, because of this status, the Service does not investigate their security status. Moreover, when an arbitrator is selected by the parties, he is retained by them and, accordingly, they must assume complete responsibility for the arbitrator's security status.

1404.4 Procedures; how to request arbitration services.

The Service prefers to act upon a joint request which should be addressed to the Director of the Federal Mediation and Conciliation Service, Washington, D.C. 20427. In the event that the request is made by only one party, the Service may act if the parties have agreed that either of them may seek a panel of arbitrators, either by specific ad hoc agreement or by specific language in the applicable collective bargaining agreement. A brief statement of the nature of the issues in dispute should accompany the request, to enable the Service to submit the names of arbitrators qualified for the issues involved. The request should also include a copy of the collective bargaining agreement or stipulation. In the event that the entire agreement is not available, a verbatim copy of the provisions relating to arbitration should accompany the request.

1404.5 Arbitrability.

Where either party claims that a dispute is not subject to arbitration, the Service will not decide the merits of such claim. The submission of a panel should not be construed as anything more than compliance with a request.

1404.6 Nomination of arbitrators.

(a) When the parties have been unable to agree on an arbitrator, the Service will submit to the parties the names of seven arbitrators unless the applicable collective bargaining agreement provides for a different number, or unless the parties themselves request a different number. Together with the submission of a panel of suggested arbitrators, the Service furnishes a short statement of the background, qualifications, experience and per diem fee of each of the nominees.

(b) In selecting names for inclusion on a panel, the Service considers many factors, but the desires of the parties are, of course, the foremost consideration. If at any time both the company and the union suggest that a name or names be omitted from a panel, such name or names will be omitted. If one party only (a company or a union) suggests that a name or names be omitted from a panel, such name or names will generally be omitted, subject to the following qualifications: (1) If the suggested omissions are excessive in number or otherwise appear to lack careful consideration, they will not be considered; (2) all such suggested omissions should be reviewed after the passage of a reasonable period of time. The Service will not place names on a panel at the request of one party unless the other party has knowledge of such request and has no objection thereto, or unless both parties join in such request. If the issue described in the request appears to require special technical experience or qualifications, arbitrators who possess such qualifications will, where possible, be included in the list submitted to the parties. Where the parties expressly request that the list be composed entirely of technicians, or that it be all-local or nonlocal, such request will be honored, if qualified arbitrators are available.

(c) Two possible methods of selection from a panel are--
(1) at a joint meeting, alternately striking names from the submitted panel until one remains, and (2) each party separately advising the Service of its order of preference by numbering each name on the panel. In almost all cases, an arbitrator is chosen from one panel of names. However, if a request for another panel is made, the Service will comply with the request, providing that additional panels are permissible under the terms of the agreement or the parties so stipulate.

(d) Subsequent adjustment of disputes is not precluded by the submission of a panel or an appointment. A substantial number of issues are being settled by the parties themselves after the initial request for a panel and after selection of the arbitrator. Notice of such settlement should be sent promptly to the arbitrator and to the Service.

(e) The arbitrator is entitled to be compensated whenever he receives insufficient notice of settlement to enable him to rearrange his schedule of arbitration hearings or working hours. In other situations, when an arbitrator spends an unusually large amount of time in arranging or rearranging hearing dates, it may be appropriate for him to make an administrative charge to the parties in the event the case is settled before hearing.

1404.7 Appointment of arbitrators.

(a) After the parties notify the Service of their selection, the arbitrator is appointed by the Director. If any party fails to notify the Service within 15 days after the date of mailing the panel, all persons named therein may be deemed acceptable to such party. The Service will make a direct appointment of an arbitrator based upon a joint request, or upon a unilateral request when the applicable collective bargaining agreement so authorizes.

(b) The arbitrator, upon appointment notification, is requested to communicate with the parties immediately to arrange for preliminary matters such as date and place of hearing.

1404.8 Status of arbitrators after appointment.

After appointment, the legal relationship of arbitrators is with the parties rather than the Service, though the Service does have a continuing interest in the proceedings. Industrial peace and good labor relations are enhanced by arbitrators who function justly, expeditiously and impartially so as to obtain and retain the respect, esteem and confidence of all participants in the arbitration proceedings. The conduct of the arbitration proceeding is under the arbitrator's jurisdiction and control, subject to such rules of procedure as the parties may jointly prescribe. He is to make his own decisions based on the record in the proceedings. The arbitrator may, unless prohibited by law, proceed in the absence of any party who, after due notice, fails to be present or to obtain a postponement. The award, however, must be supported by evidence.

1404.9 Prompt decision.

(a) Early hearing and decision of industrial disputes is desirable in the interest of good labor relations. The parties should inform the Service whenever a decision is unduly delayed. The Service expects to be notified by the arbitrator if and when (1) he cannot schedule, hear and determine issues promptly, and (2) he is advised that a dispute has been settled by the parties prior to arbitration.

(b) The award shall be made not later than 30 days from the date of the closing of the hearing, or the receipt of a transcript and any post-hearing briefs, or if oral hearings have been waived, then from the date of receipt of the final statements and proof by the arbitrator, unless otherwise agreed upon by the parties or specified by law. However, a failure to make such an award within 30 days shall not invalidate an award.

1404.10 Arbitrator's award and report.

(a) At the conclusion of the hearing and after the award has been submitted to the parties, each arbitrator is required to file a copy with the Service. The arbitrator is further required to submit a report showing a breakdown of his fees and expense charges so that the Service may be in a position to check conformance with its fee policies. Cooperation in filing both award and report within 15 days after handing down the award is expected of all arbitrators.

(b) It is the policy of the Service not to release arbitration decisions for publication without the consent of both parties. Furthermore, the Service expects the arbitrators it has nominated or appointed not to give publicity to awards they may issue, except in a manner agreeable to both parties.

1404.11 Fees of arbitrators.

(a) No administrative or filing fee is charged by the Service. The current policy of the Service permits each of its nominees or appointees to charge a per diem fee for his services, the amount of which is certified in advance by him to the Service. Each arbitrator's maximum per diem fee is set forth on his biographical sketch which is sent to the parties at such time as his name is submitted to them for consideration. The arbitrator shall not change his per diem fee without giving at least 90 days advance notice to the Service of his intention to do so.

(b) In those rare instances where arbitrators fix wages or other important terms of a new contract, the maximum fee noted above may be exceeded by the arbitrator after agreement by the parties. Conversely, an arbitrator may give due consideration to the financial condition of the parties and charge less than his usual fee in appropriate cases.

1404.12 Conduct of hearings.

The Service does not prescribe detailed or specific rules of procedure for the conduct of an arbitration proceeding because it favors flexibility in labor relations. Questions such as hearing rooms, submission of prehearing or posthearing briefs, and recording of testimony, are left to the discretion of the individual arbitrator and to the parties. The Service does, however, expect its arbitrators and the parties to conform to applicable laws, and to be guided by ethical and procedural standards as codified by appropriate professional organizations and generally accepted by the industrial community and experienced arbitrators.

In cities where the Service maintains offices, the parties are welcome upon request to the Service to use its conference rooms when they are available.

Appendix B

AMERICAN ARBITRATION ASSOCIATION VOLUNTARY LABOR ARBITRATION RULES

Agreement of Parties—The parties shall be deemed to have made these Rules a part of their arbitration agreement whenever, in a collective bargaining agreement or submission, they have provided for arbitration by the American Arbitration Association (hereinafter AAA) or under its Rules. These Rules shall apply in the form obtaining at the time the arbitration is initiated.

Name of Tribunal—Any Tribunal constituted by the parties under these Rules shall be called the Voluntary Labor Arbitration Tribunal.

Administrator—When parties agree to arbitrate under these Rules and an arbitration is instituted thereunder, they thereby authorize the AAA to administer the arbitration. The authority and obligations of the Administrator are as provided in the agreement of the parties and in these Rules.

Delegation of Duties—The duties of the AAA may be carried out through such representatives or committees as the AAA may direct.

National Panel of Labor Arbitrators—The AAA shall establish and maintain a National Panel of Labor Arbitrators and shall appoint arbitrators therefrom, as hereinafter provided.

Office of Tribunal—The general office of the Labor Arbitration Tribunal is the headquarters of the AAA, which may, however, assign the administration of an arbitration to any of its Regional Offices.

Initiation Under an Arbitration Clause in a Collective Bargaining Agreement—Arbitration under an arbitration clause in a collective bargaining agreement under these Rules may be initiated by either party in the following manner:

(a) By giving written notice to the other party of intention to arbitrate (Demand), which notice shall contain a statement setting forth the nature of the dispute and the remedy sought, and

(b) By filing at any Regional Office of the AAA three copies of said notice, together with a copy of the collective bargaining agreement, or such parts thereof as relate to the dispute, including the arbitration provisions. After the Arbitrator is appointed, no new or different claim may be submitted to him except with the consent of the Arbitrator and all other parties.

Answer—The party upon whom the demand for arbitration is made may file an answering statement with the AAA within seven days after notice from the AAA, in which event he shall simultaneously send a copy of his answer to the other party. If no answer is filed within the stated time, it will be assumed that the claim is denied. Failure to file an answer shall not operate to delay the arbitration.

Initiation under a Submission—Parties to any collective bargaining agreement may initiate an arbitration under these Rules by filing at any Regional Office of the AAA two copies of a written agreement to arbitrate under these Rules (Submission), signed by the parties and setting forth the nature of the dispute and the remedy sought.

10. **Fixing of Locale**—The parties may mutually agree upon the locale where the arbitration is to be held. If the locale is not designated in the collective bargaining agreement or submission, and if there is a dispute as to the appropriate locale, the AAA shall have the power to determine the locale and its decision shall be binding.

11. **Qualifications of Arbitrator**—No person shall serve as a neutral Arbitrator in any arbitration in which he has any financial or personal interest in the result of the arbitration, unless the parties, in writing, waive such disqualification.

12. **Appointment from Panel**—If the parties have not appointed an Arbitrator and have not provided any other method of appointment, the Arbitrator shall be appointed in the following manner: Immediately after the filing of the Demand or Submission, the AAA shall submit simultaneously to each party an identical list of names of persons chosen from the Labor Panel. Each party shall have seven days from the mailing date in which to cross off any names to which he objects, number the remaining names indicating the order of his preference, and return the list to the AAA. If a party does not return the list within the time specified, all persons named therein shall be deemed acceptable. From among the persons who have been approved on both lists, and in accordance with the designated order of mutual preference, the AAA shall invite the acceptance of an Arbitrator to serve. If the parties fail to agree upon any of the persons named or if those named decline or are unable to act, or if for any other reason the appointment cannot be made from the submitted lists, the Administrator shall have power to make the appointment from other members of the Panel without the submission of any additional lists.

13. **Direct Appointment by Parties**—If the agreement of the parties names an Arbitrator or specifies a method of appointing an Arbitrator, that designation or method shall be followed. The notice of appointment, with the name and address of such Arbitrator, shall be filed with the AAA by the appointing party.

If the agreement specifies a period of time within which an Arbitrator shall be appointed, and any party fails to make such appointment within that period, the AAA may make the appointment.

If no period of time is specified in the agreement, the AAA shall notify the parties to make the appointment and if within seven days thereafter such Arbitrator has not been so appointed, the AAA shall make the appointment.

14. **Appointment of Neutral Arbitrator by Party-Appointed Arbitrators**—If the parties have appointed their Arbitrators, or if either or both of them have been appointed as provided in Section 13, and have authorized such Arbitrators to appoint a neutral Arbitrator within a specified time and no appointment is made within such time or any agreed extension thereof, the AAA may appoint a neutral Arbitrator, who shall act as Chairman.

If no period of time is specified for appointment of the neutral Arbitrator and the parties do not make the appointment within seven days from the date of the appointment of the last party-appointed Arbitrator, the AAA shall appoint such neutral Arbitrator, who shall act as Chairman.

If the parties have agreed that the Arbitrators shall appoint the neutral Arbitrator from the Panel, the AAA shall furnish to the party-appointed Arbitrators, in the manner prescribed in Section 12, a list selected from the Panel, and the appointment of the neutral Arbitrator shall be made as prescribed in such Section.

15. **Number of Arbitrators**—If the arbitration agreement does not specify the number of Arbitrators, the dispute shall be heard and determined by one Arbitrator, unless the parties otherwise agree.

16. **Notice to Arbitrator of His Appointment**—Notice of the appointment of the neutral Arbitrator shall be mailed to the Arbitrator by the AAA and the signed acceptance of the Arbitrator shall be filed with the AAA prior to the opening of the first hearing.

17. **Disclosure by Arbitrator of Disqualification**—Prior to accepting his appointment, the prospective neutral Arbitrator shall disclose any circumstances likely to create a presumption of bias or which he believes might disqualify him as an impartial Arbitrator. Upon receipt of such information, the AAA shall immediately disclose it to the parties. If either party declines to waive the presumptive disqualification, the vacancy thus created shall be filled in accordance with the applicable provisions of these Rules.

18. **Vacancies**—If any Arbitrator should resign, die, withdraw, refuse or be unable or disqualified to perform the duties of his office, the AAA shall, on proof satisfactory to it, declare the office vacant. Vacancies shall be filled in the same manner as that governing the making of the original appointment, and the matter shall be reheard by the new Arbitrator.

19. **Time and Place of Hearing**—The Arbitrator shall fix the time and place for each hearing. At least five days prior thereto the AAA shall mail notice of the time and place of hearing to each party, unless the parties otherwise agree.

20. **Representation by Counsel**—Any party may be represented at the hearing by counsel or by other authorized representative.

21. **Stenographic Record**—Whenever a stenographic record is requested by one or more parties, the AAA will arrange for a stenographer. The total cost of the record shall be shared equally among parties ordering copies, unless they agree otherwise.

22. **Attendance at Hearings**—Persons having a direct interest in the arbitration are entitled to attend hearings. The Arbitrator shall have the power to require the retirement of any witness or witnesses during the testimony of other witnesses. It shall be discretionary with the Arbitrator to determine the propriety of the attendance of any other persons.

23. **Adjournments**—The Arbitrator for good cause shown may adjourn the hearing upon the request of a party or upon his own initiative, and shall adjourn when all the parties agree thereto.

24. **Oaths**—Before proceeding with the first hearing, each Arbitrator may take an Oath of Office, and if required by law, shall do so. The Arbitrator may, in his discretion, require witnesses to testify under oath administered by any duly qualified person, and if required by law or requested by either party, shall do so.

25. **Majority Decision**—Whenever there is more than one

Arbitrator, all decisions of the Arbitrators shall be majority vote. The award shall also be made by majori vote unless the concurrence of all is expressly require

26. **Order of Proceedings**—A hearing shall be opened the filing of the oath of the Arbitrator, where require and by the recording of the place, time and date hearing, the presence of the Arbitrator and parties, a counsel if any, and the receipt by the Arbitrator of t Demand and answer, if any, or the Submission.

Exhibits, when offered by either party, may be r ceived in evidence by the Arbitrator. The names a addresses of all witnesses and exhibits in order receiv shall be made a part of the record.

The Arbitrator may, in his discretion, vary the norm procedure under which the initiating party first presen his claim, but in any case shall afford full and equ opportunity to all parties for presentation of releva proofs.

27. **Arbitration in the Absence of a Party**—Unless t law provides to the contrary, the arbitration may pr ceed in the absence of any party, who, after due notic fails to be present or fails to obtain an adjournmen An award shall not be made solely on the default of party. The Arbitrator shall require the other party submit such evidence as he may require for the makin of an award.

28. **Evidence**—The parties may offer such evidence they desire and shall produce such additional eviden as the Arbitrator may deem necessary to an unde standing and determination of the dispute. When t Arbitrator is authorized by law to subpoena witness and documents, he may do so upon his own initiativ or upon the request of any party. The Arbitrator sha be the judge of the relevancy and materiality of t evidence offered and conformity to legal rules of ev dence shall not be necessary. All evidence shall be take in the presence of all of the Arbitrators and all of t parties except where any of the parties is absent default or has waived his right to be present.

29. **Evidence by Affidavit and Filing of Documents**—Th Arbitrator may receive and consider the evidence witnesses by affidavit, but shall give it only such weig as he deems proper after consideration of any obje tions made to its admission.

All documents not filed with the Arbitrator at th hearing but which are arranged at the hearing or sub sequently by agreement of the parties to be submitte shall be filed with the AAA for transmission to th Arbitrator. All parties shall be afforded opportunit to examine such documents.

30. **Inspection**—Whenever the Arbitrator deems it nec essary, he may make an inspection in connection wit the subject matter of the dispute after written notic to the parties who may, if they so desire, be present such inspection.

31. **Closing of Hearings**—The Arbitrator shall inquir of all parties whether they have any further proofs offer or witnesses to be heard. Upon receiving negativ replies, the Arbitrator shall declare the hearings close and a minute thereof shall be recorded. If briefs o other documents are to be filed, the hearings shall b declared closed as of the final date set by the Arbitrato for filing with the AAA. The time limit within whic the Arbitrator is required to make his award shall com mence to run, in the absence of other agreement by th parties, upon the closing of the hearings.

32. **Reopening of Hearings**—The hearings may be re opened by the Arbitrator on his own motion, or on th motion of either party, for good cause shown, at an

e before the award is made, but if the reopening of
hearing would prevent the making of the award
thin the specific time agreed upon by the parties in
contract out of which the controversy has arisen,
matter may not be reopened, unless both parties
ree upon the extension of such time limit. When no
ecific date is fixed in the contract, the Arbitrator
y reopen the hearings, and the Arbitrator shall have
days from the closing of the reopened hearings with-
which to make an award.

Waiver of Rules—Any party who proceeds with the
bitration after knowledge that any provision or re-
rement of these Rules has not been complied with
d who fails to state his objection thereto in writing,
all be deemed to have waived his right to object.

Waiver of Oral Hearing—The parties may provide,
written agreement, for the waiver of oral hearings.
the parties are unable to agree as to the procedure,
AAA shall specify a fair and equitable procedure.

Extensions of Time—The parties may modify any
riod of time by mutual agreement. The AAA for good
ise may extend any period of time established by
se Rules, except the time for making the award. The
.A shall notify the parties of any such extension of
ie and its reason therefor.

Serving of Notices—Each party to a Submission or
ier agreement which provides for arbitration under
se Rules shall be deemed to have consented and shall
asent that any papers, notices or process necessary
proper for the initiation or continuation of an ar-
ration under these Rules and for any court action in
nnection therewith or the entry of judgment on an
ard made thereunder, may be served upon such party
) by mail addressed to such party or his attorney
his last known address, or (b) by personal service,
thin or without the state wherein the arbitration is
be held.

Time of Award—The award shall be rendered
omptly by the Arbitrator and, unless otherwise agreed
the parties, or specified by the law, not later than
rty days from the date of closing the hearings, or
oral hearings have been waived, then from the date
transmitting the final statements and proofs to the
bitrator.

Form of Award—The award shall be in writing and
all be signed either by the neutral Arbitrator or by a
icurring majority if there be more than one Ar-
rator. The parties shall advise the AAA whenever
ey do not require the Arbitrator to accompany the
ard with an opinion.

Award Upon Settlement—If the parties settle their
spute during the course of the arbitration, the Ar-
rator, upon their request, may set forth the terms of
e agreed settlement in an award.

Delivery of Award to Parties—Parties shall accept
legal delivery of the award the placing of the award
a true copy thereof in the mail by the AAA, ad-
essed to such party at his last known address or to his
attorney, or personal service of the award, or the filing
of the award in any manner which may be prescribed
by law.

41. Release of Documents for Judicial Proceedings—The
AAA shall, upon the written request of a party, furnish
to such party at his expense certified facsimiles of any
papers in the AAA's possession that may be required in
judicial proceedings relating to the arbitration.

42. Judicial Proceedings—The AAA is not a necessary
party in judicial proceedings relating to the arbitration.

43. Administrative Fee—As a nonprofit organization,
the AAA shall prescribe an administrative fee schedule
to compensate it for the cost of providing administrative services. The schedule in effect at the time of filing
shall be applicable.

44. Expenses—The expenses of witnesses for either side
shall be paid by the party producing such witnesses.

Expenses of the arbitration, other than the cost of
the stenographic record, including required traveling
and other expenses of the Arbitrator and of AAA representatives, and the expenses of any witnesses or the
cost of any proofs produced at the direct request of the
Arbitrator, shall be borne equally by the parties unless
they agree otherwise, or unless the Arbitrator in his
award assesses such expenses or any part thereof
against any specified party or parties.

45. Communication with Arbitrator—There shall be no
communication between the parties and a neutral Arbitrator other than at oral hearings. Any other oral or
written communications from the parties to the Arbitrator shall be directed to the AAA for transmittal
to the Arbitrator.

46. Interpretation and Application of Rules—The Arbitrator shall interpret and apply these Rules insofar
as they relate to his powers and duties. When there is
more than one Arbitrator and a difference arises among
them concerning the meaning or application of any such
Rules, it shall be decided by majority vote. If that is
unobtainable, either Arbitrator or party may refer the
question to the AAA for final decision. All other Rules
shall be interpreted and applied by the AAA.

ADMINISTRATIVE FEE SCHEDULE

Initial Administrative Fee: The initial administrative
fee is $50.00 for each party, due and payable at the
time of filing.

Additional Hearings: A fee of $25.00 is payable by each
party for each second and subsequent hearing which is
either clerked by the AAA or held in a hearing room
provided by the AAA.

Postponement Fees: A fee of $5.00 is payable by a
party causing a postponement of any scheduled hearing.

Appendix C

RESPONSIBILITY OF THE MEDIATOR

1 | **The Responsibility of the Mediator to the Parties**

The primary responsibility for the resolution of a labor dispute rests upon the parties themselves. The mediator at all times should recognize that the agreements reached in collective bargaining are voluntarily made by the parties. It is the mediator's responsibility to assist the parties in reaching a settlement.

It is desirable that agreement be reached by collective bargaining without mediation assistance. However, public policy and applicable statutes recognize that mediation is the appropriate form of governmental participation in cases where it is required. Whether and when a mediator should intercede will normally be influenced by the desires of the parties. Intercession by a mediator on his own motion should be limited to exceptional cases.

The mediator must not consider himself limited to keeping peace at the bargaining table. His role should be one of being a resource upon which the parties may draw and, when appropriate, he should be prepared to provide both procedural and substantive suggestions and alternatives which will assist the parties in successful negotiations.

Since mediation is essentially a voluntary process, the acceptability of the mediator by the parties as a person of integrity, objectivity, and fairness is absolutely essential to the effective performance of the duties of the mediator. The manner in which the mediator carries out his professional duties and responsibilities will measure his usefulness as a mediator. The quality of his character as well as his intellectual, emotional, social and technical attributes will reveal themselves by the conduct of the mediator and his oral and written communications with the parties, other mediators and the public.

2 | **The Responsibility of the Mediator Toward Other Mediators**

A mediator should not enter any dispute which is being mediated by another mediator or mediators without first conferring with the person or persons conducting such mediation. The mediator should not intercede in a dispute merely because another mediator may also be participating. Conversely, it should not be assumed that the lack of mediation participation by one mediator indicates a need for participation by another mediator.

In those situations where more than one mediator is participating in a particular case, each mediator has a responsibility to keep the others informed of developments essential to a cooperative effort and should extend every possible courtesy to his fellow mediator.

The mediator should carefully avoid any appearance of disagreement with or criticism of his fellow mediator. Discussions as to what positions and actions mediators should take in particular cases should be carried on solely between or among the mediators.

3 | **The Responsibility of the Mediator Toward His Agency and His Profession**

Agencies responsible for providing mediation assistance to parties engaged in collective bargaining are a part of government. The mediator must recognize that, as such, he is part of government. The mediator should constantly bear in mind that he and his work are not judged solely on an individual

143

basis but that he is also judged as a representative of his agency. Any improper conduct or professional shortcoming, therefore, reflects not only on the individual mediator but upon his employer and, as such, jeopardizes the effectiveness of his agency, other government agencies, and the acceptability of the mediation process.

The mediator should not use his position for private gain or advantage, nor should he engage in any employment, activity, or enterprise which will conflict with his work as a mediator, nor should he accept any money or thing of value for the performance of his duties—other than his regular salary—or incur obligations to any party which might interfere with the impartial performance of his duties.

4 | The Responsibility of the Mediator Toward the Public

Collective bargaining is in essence a private, voluntary process. The primary purpose of mediation is to assist the parties to achieve a settlement. Such assistance does not abrogate the rights of the parties to resort to economic and legal sanctions. However, the mediation process may include a responsibility to assert the interest of the public that a particular dispute be settled; that a work stoppage be ended; and that normal operations be resumed. It should be understood, however, that the mediator does not regulate or control any of the content of a collective bargaining agreement.

It is conceivable that a mediator might find it necessary to withdraw from a negotiation, if it is patently clear that the parties intend to use his presence as implied governmental sanction for an agreement obviously contrary to public policy.

It is recognized that labor disputes are settled at the bargaining table; however, the mediator may release appropriate information with due regard (1) to the desires of the parties, (2) to whether that information will assist or impede the settlement of the dispute and (3) to the needs of an informed public.

Publicity shall not be used by a mediator to enhance his own position or that of his agency. Where two or more mediators are mediating a dispute, public information should be handled through a mutually agreeable procedure.

5 | The Responsibility of the Mediator Toward the Mediation Process

Collective bargaining is an established institution in our economic way of life. The practice of mediation requires the development of alternatives which the parties will voluntarily accept as a basis for settling their problems. Improper pressures which jeopardize voluntary action by the parties should not be a part of mediation.

Since the status, experience, and ability of the mediator lend weight to his suggestions and recommendations, he should evaluate carefully the effect of his suggestions and recommendations and accept full responsibility for their honesty and merit.

The mediator has a continuing responsibility to study industrial relations to improve his skills and upgrade his abilities.

Suggestions by individual mediators or agencies to parties, which give the implication that transfer of a case from one mediation "forum" to another will produce better results, are unprofessional and are to be condemned.

Confidential information acquired by the mediator should not be disclosed to others for any purpose or in a legal proceeding or be used directly or indirectly for the personal benefit or profit of the mediator.

Bargaining positions, proposals, or suggestions given to the mediator in confidence during the course of bargaining for his sole information should not be disclosed to the other party without first securing permission from the party or person who gave it to him.

Appendix D

OPERATIONS MANUAL SECTION 2102

III. FMCS Policy

The Service may offer its services in any labor-management grievance dispute (except airlines and railroads) where interstate commerce can be affected. If the Service enters the dispute, the regional director may assign in writing a mediator on either of the following bases:

A. For Mediation
Such an assignment is without limitation as to the extent of participation if the case may be properly classified in the "exceptional and last resort" category under the terms of the Act . Note that a case must be both "exceptional" and "last resort" before it may be properly classified in this category.

B. Limited Mediation
Such an assignment is limited participation for the purpose of suggesting and inducing agreement on procedures or machinery for settlement, but not for the purpose of mediating the basic issues involved or for considering the merits thereof. This type of assignment can be normally made when the grievance dispute affects interstate commerce so as to justify a mediation assignment, but fails to qualify as "exceptional and last resort. "

IV. Definitions

The Service interprets the terms exceptional, last resort, and grievance disputes as follows:

A. Exceptional
Of special importance because of the essential nature of the products of the involved employing establishment to Government contracts or operations, to defense production, to interstate commerce, to the economy as a whole, to related and involved indus-

tries, or to the general health, safety, and welfare of a community or the public, either locally or nationally.

B. Last Resort

No other adequate facility or procedure is available which can prevent a disruption to production, and assist in maintaining sound labor-management relations.

C. Grievance Disputes

Labor-management disputes arising over the application or interpretation of an existing collective bargaining agreement. Labor-management disputes which do not directly involve the application or interpretation of an existing collective bargaining agreement are not grievances within the meaning of the Act, even-though they may be designated as grievances by one or both of the disputing parties.

V. Internal Procedures

A. In grievance dispute cases where Service participation is "without limitation," mediators shall utilize any and all mediation and conciliation techniques to bring the disputants into agreement.

B. On assignments for "limited mediation" of grievance dispute cases the mediator should usually urge the parties to utilize the grievance or arbitration procedures in their collective bargaining contract, if the contract contains such provisions. If the contract lacks adequate procedures, he should urge them to agree upon a procedure for settling the immediate issue in dispute. If successful, the mediator should close the case with the regular final report, indicating the method of settlement. But if limited mediation fails, the mediator shall send to his regional director a complete written report which will serve as a basis for classifying a dispute as "exceptional and last resort" as well as for planning future action. After reviewing the report, the regional director must decide whether to withdraw the mediator and close the case, or to amend the assignment to authorize participation without limitation.

VI. Effect of Contract Provisions and Joint Agreements

The Service cannot be bound by contract provisions or joint agreements requiring the Service to mediate grievance disputes or to perform any other act or service except as authorized by existing law, official regulations, and policies. It does not matter that the parties may have agreed upon mediation by the Service as a method for settlement of grievances. The Service shall make its conciliation and mediation services available in the settlement of such disputes on the same basis as if the agreement did not provide for the Service to intervene in the grievance procedure. If such a provision is proposed for inclusion in a collective bargaining agreement, the mediator must tactfully inform the parties of the policy of the Service as outlined in these Operating Procedures; and that the Service must reserve the right to determine, in accordance with its general policies, whether it will intervene in each grievance dispute.

Appendix E

TITLE II—CONCILIATION OF LABOR DISPUTES IN INDUSTRIES AFFECTING COMMERCE; NATIONAL EMERGENCIES

SEC. 201.   That it is the policy of the United States that—

(a) sound and stable industrial peace and the advancement of the general welfare, health, and safety of the Nation and of the best interest of employers and employees can most satisfactorily be secured by the settlement of issues between employers and employees through the processes of conference and collective bargaining between employers and the representatives of their employees;

(b) the settlement of issues between employers and employees through collective bargaining may be advanced by making available full and adequate governmental facilities for conciliation, mediation, and voluntary arbitration to aid and encourage employers and the representatives of their employees to reach and maintain agreements concerning rates of pay, hours, and working conditions, and to make all reasonable efforts to settle their differences by mutual agreement reached through conferences and collective bargaining or by such methods as may be provided for in any applicable agreement for the settlement of disputes; and

(c) certain controversies which arise between parties to collective-bargaining agreements may be avoided or minimized by making available full and adequate governmental facilities for furnishing assistance to employers and the representatives of their employees in formulating for inclusion within such agreements provision for adequate notice of any proposed changes in the terms of such agreements, for the final adjustment of grievances or questions regarding the application or interpretation of such agreements, and other provisions designed to prevent the subsequent arising of such controversies.

SEC. 202.   (a) There is hereby created an independent agency to be known as the Federal Mediation and Conciliation Service (herein referred to as the "Service," except that for sixty days after the date of the enactment of this Act such term shall refer to the Conciliation Service of the Department of Labor).   The Service

149

shall be under the direction of a Federal Mediation and Conciliation Director (hereinafter referred to as the "Director"), who shall be appointed by the President by and with the advice and consent of the Senate. The Director shall receive compensation at the rate of $12,000* per annum. The Director shall not engage in any other business, vocation, or employment.

(b) The Director is authorized, subject to the civil-service laws, to appoint such clerical and other personnel as may be necessary for the execution of the functions of the Service, and shall fix their compensation in accordance with the Classification Act of 1923, as amended, and may, without regard to the provisions of the civil-service laws and the Classification Act of 1923, as amended, appoint and fix the compensation of such conciliators and mediators as may be necessary to carry out the functions of the Service. The Director is authorized to make such expenditures for supplies, facilities, and services as he deems necessary. Such expenditures shall be allowed and paid upon presentation of itemized vouchers therefor approved by the Director or by any employee designated by him for that purpose.

(c) The principal office of the Service shall be in the District of Columbia, but the Director may establish regional offices convenient to localities in which labor controversies are likely to arise. The Director may by order, subject to revocation at any time, delegate any authority and discretion conferred upon him by this Act to any regional director, or other officer or employee of the Service. The Director may establish suitable procedures for cooperation with State and local mediation agencies. The Director shall make an annual report in writing to Congress at the end of the fiscal year.

(d) All mediation and conciliation functions of the Secretary of Labor or the United States Conciliation Service under section 8 of the Act entitled "An Act to create a Department of Labor," approved March 4, 1913 (U.S.C., title 29, sec. 51), and all functions of the United States Conciliation Service under any other law are hereby transferred to the Federal Mediation and Conciliation Service, together with the personnel and records of the United States Conciliation Service. Such transfer shall take effect upon the sixtieth day after the date of enactment of this Act. Such transfer shall not affect any proceedings pending before the United States Conciliation Service or any certification, order, rule, or regulation theretofore made by it or by the Secretary of Labor. The Director and the Service shall not be subject in any way to the jurisdiction or authority of the Secretary of labor or any official or division of the Department of Labor.

FUNCTIONS OF THE SERVICE

SEC. 203. (a) It shall be the duty of the Service, in order to prevent or minimize interruptions of the free flow of commerce growing out of labor disputes, to assist parties to labor disputes in industries affecting commerce to settle such disputes through conciliation and mediation.

(b) The Service may proffer its services in any labor dispute in any industry affecting commerce, either upon its own motion or upon the request of one or more of the parties to the dispute, whenever in its judgment such dispute threatens to cause a substantial interruption of commerce. The Director and the Service are directed to avoid attempting to mediate disputes which would have only a minor effect on interstate commerce if State or other conciliation services are available to the parties. Whenever the Service does proffer its services in any dispute, it shall be the duty of the Service promptly to put itself in communication

*Pursuant to Public Law 88–426, 88th Congress, 2d Session, Title III, approved August 14, 1964, the salary of the Director shall be $27,000 per year.

150

SEC. 206. Whenever in the opinion of the President of the United States, a threatened or actual strike or lock-out affecting an entire industry or a substantial part thereof engaged in trade, commerce, transportation, transmission, or communi-

Appendix F

PART 1401--AVAILABILITY OF
INFORMATION
PART 1402--PROCEDURES OF THE
SERVICE
PART 1403--FUNCTIONS AND DUTIES
PART 1404--ARBITRATION

Revisions of Regulations

Parts 1401 through 1404 of chapter XII are revised to read
as follows:

PART 1401--AVAILABILITY OF
INFORMATION

Sec.
1401.1   Places at which information may be obtained.
1401.2   Nondisclosure of information.
1401.3   Confidential records.
1401.4   Notices of disputes nonconfidential.
1401.5   Compliance with subpoenas.

AUTHORITY: The provisions of this Part 1401 issued under
sec. 202, 61 Stat. 153, as amended; 29 U.S.C. 172. Interpret
or apply sec. 3, 80 Stat. 250, sec. 203, 61 Stat. 153; 5 U.S.C.
552, 29 U.S.C. 173.

1401.1 Places at which information may be obtained.

Any individual employer or union, or representative thereof,
desiring information regarding the operations of the Service within
a region should communicate with the regional office of the Service in the region in which the labor dispute or other matter exists with respect to which information is sought. General inquiries for information concerning the Service should be addressed

to the Federal Mediation and Conciliation Service, 14th and Constitution Avenue NW., Washington, D.C. 20427. The location of regional offices of the Service and their respective jurisdictions are as follows:

Region Number, Address, and Jurisdiction

1. Room 1101, 11th Floor East, 346 Broadway, New York, N.Y. 10013--Maine; New Hampshire; Vermont; Connecticut; Rhode Island; Massachusetts; New York; and northern New Jersey counties of Bergen, Essex, Hudson, Middlesex, Morris, Passaic, Somerset, Sussex, and Union.

2. Room 5021, U.S. Courthouse and Post Office Building, Ninth and Chestnut Streets, Philadelphia, Pa. 19107--Pennsylvania; Delaware; Maryland; District of Columbia; West Virginia; southern New Jersey counties of Atlantic, Burlington, Camden, Cape May, Cumberland, Gloucester, Ocean, Warren, Hunterdon, Mercer, Monmouth, and Salem; eastern Virginia counties of Alleghany, Botetourt, Roanoake, Franklin, Henry, and all east of these counties; and southeastern Ohio counties of Belmont, Monroe, Washington, Noble, and Guernsey.

3. Room 154, Peachtree at Seventh Street Building, 50 Seventh Street NE., Atlanta, Ga. 30323--western Virginia counties of Lee, Wise, Scott, Dickenson, Buchanan, Russell, Washington, Tazewill, Smyth, Bland, Wythe, Grayson, Carroll, Pulaski, Giles, Craig, Montgomery, Floyd, and Patrick; southwest Kentucky counties of Fulton, Hickman, Carlisle, Ballare, McCracken, Graves, Marshall, Calloway, Livingston, Todd, Lyon, Trigg, Caldwell, Crittenden, Union, Webster, Hopkins, Christian, Muhlenberg, Logan, and Simpson; Arkansas (Crittenden County only); Tennessee; North Carolina; South Carolina; Georgia; Florida; Alabama; Mississippi; Louisiana; Puerto Rico; and the Virgin Islands.

4. Room 2031, Superior Building, 815 Superior Avenue NE., Cleveland, Ohio 44114--Indiana (counties of Clark and Floyd); Kentucky (except the counties under Region 3 jurisdiction); Ohio (except the counties of Belmont, Monroe, Washington, Noble, and Guernsey); Michigan (Lower Peninsula; Upper Peninsula under Region 5 jurisdiction).

5. Room 1402, U.S. Courthouse and Federal Office Building, 219 South Dearborn Street, Chicago, Ill. 60604--Illinois (except the counties under Region 6 jurisdiction); Indiana (except Clark and Floyd Counties under Region 4 jurisdiction); Wisconsin; Minnesota; North Dakota; South Dakota; and Michigan (Upper Peninsula; Lower Peninsula under Region 4 jurisdiction).

6. Room 3266, Federal Building. 1520 Market Street, St. Louis, Mo. 63103--Iowa; Missouri; southwest Illinois (counties of Calhoun, Greene, Jersey, Madison, Macoupin, Monroe, Randolph and St. Clair); Arkansas (except Crittenden County); Nebraska; Kansas; Oklahoma; and Texas (except El Paso and Hudspeth Counties under Region 7 jurisdiction).

7. Room 13471, New Federal Office Building, 450 Golden Gate Avenue, Post Office Box 36007, San Francisco, Calif. 94102 --Washington; Oregon; California; Idaho; Montana; Wyoming; Nevada; Utah; Colorado; Arizona; New Mexico; southwest Texas (counties of El Paso and Hudspeth); Alaska; Hawaii; and Guam.

1401.2 Nondisclosure of information.

Public policy and the successful effectuation of the Federal Mediation and Conciliation Service's mission require that commissioners and employees maintain a reputation for impartiality and integrity. Labor and management or other interested parties participating in mediation efforts must have the assurance and confidence that information disclosed to commissioners and other employees of the service will not subsequently be divulged, voluntarily or because of compulsion.

1401.3 Confidential records.

All files, reports, letters, memoranda, minutes, documents, or other papers (hereinafter referred to as "confidential records") in the official custody of the Service or any of its employees, relating to or acquired in its or their official activities under Title II of the Labor-Management Relations Act, 1947, as amended, are hereby declared to be confidential. No such confidential records shall be disclosed to any unauthorized person, or be taken or withdrawn, copied or removed from the custody of the Service or its employees by any person, or by any agent or representative of such person without the prior consent of the Director.

1401.4 Notices of dispute nonconfidential.

Written notices of disputes received pursuant to section 8 (d)(3) of the Labor-Management Relations Act, 1947, as amended, are not confidential records of the Service. Parties at interest have the right to receive certified copies of any such notice of dispute upon written request to the regional director of the region in which the notice is filed. The notice of dispute and a conformed copy should be filed in the office of the regional director of the region in which the dispute exists, or if the filing party so desires, at the office of the Director of the Service; and if the dispute is occurring in two or more regions such notice may be filed with the regional director for any of such regions, or filed at the office of the Director of the Service, at 14th and Constitution Avenue NW., Washington, D.C. 20427. A conformed copy of such notice of dispute should be served upon the other party to the contract.

1401.5 Compliance with subpoenas.

No officer, employee, or other person officially connected in any capacity with the Service, shall produce or present any confidential records of the Service or testify on behalf of any party to any cause pending in any arbitration or other proceedings or court or before any board, commission, committee, tribunal, investigatory body, or administrative agency of the United States or of any State, Territory, the District of Columbia or any municipality with respect to facts or other matters coming to his knowledge in his official capacity or with respect to the contents of any confidential records of the Service, whether in answer to an order, subpoena, subpoena duces tecum, or otherwise, without the prior written consent of the Director. Whenever any subpoena duces tecum calling for confidential records or testimony as described above shall have been served upon any such officer, employee, or other person, he will appear in answer thereto, and unless otherwise expressly directed by the Director, respectfully decline, by reason of this section, to produce or present such confidential records or to give such testimony.

Appendix G

FMCS Form F-7
Rev. May 1964
Ch-2003 O/M-C/H

Form Approved
Budget Bureau . 23-R001.10

NOTICE TO MEDIATION AGENCIES

To: Regional Office, <u>FEDERAL MEDIATION AND CONCILIATION SERVICE</u>; and
United States Government

To: _____   Date _____
(Appropriate State or Territorial agency)

You are hereby notified that written notice of the proposed termination or modification of the existing collective bargaining contract was served upon the other party to this contract and that no agreement has been reached.

·1. (a) Name of employer_____ Phone No. _____
(If more than one company or an association, submit names and addresses on separate sheet in duplicate)

Address of establishment affected_____
(Street)   (City)   (State)   (Zip Code)
(If more than one establishment, or plant, list addresses on separate sheet)

(b) Employer Official to communicate with _____· Phone No. _____
(Name and Title)

Address_____
(Street)   (City)   (State)   (Zip Code)

2. (a) International union and Local No. _____ Phone No. _____

Address of local union _____
(Street)   (City)   (State)   (Zip Code)

(b) Union Official to communicate with _____ Phone No. _____

Address _____
(Street)   (City)   (State)   (Zip Code)

3. (a) Number of employees covered by the Contract(s) _____

(b) Total number employed by the Company at this location(s) _____

4.   Type of establishment and principal products, or services_____

_____
(Factory, mine, wholesaler, over-the-road trucking, etc.)

5.   (a) Contract expiration or reopening date _____

6.   Name of official filing this notice _____ Title _____

Address_____ Phone No. _____

Check on whose behalf this notice is filed: Union _____ Employer _____

Signature _____

Receipt of this notice does not constitute a request for mediation nor does it commit the agencies to offer their facilities. This particular form of notice is not legally required. Receipt of notice will not be acknowledged in writing by the Federal Mediation and Conciliation Service.

(Attach copies of any statement you wish to make to the Mediation Agencies.)

(See list on reverse of copy 6)

Appendix H

Section 8 (d). Labor Managment Relations Act

Provided, that where there is in effect a collective-bargaining contract covering employees in an industry affecting commerce, the duty to bargain collectively shall also mean that no party to such contract, shall terminate or modify such contract, unless the party desiring such termination or modification--

(1) serves a written notice upon the other party to the contract of the proposed termination or modification sixty days prior to the expiration date thereof, or in the event such contract contains no expiration date, sixty days prior to the time it is pro - posed to make such termination or modification;

(2) offers to meet and confer with the other party for the purpose of negotiating a new contract or a contract containing the proposed modifications;

(3) notifies the Federal Mediation and Conciliation Service within thirty days after such notice of the existence of a dispute, and simultaneously therewith notifies any State or Territorial a - gency established to mediate and conciliate disputes within the State or Territory where the dispute occurred, provided no agree - ment has been reached by that time; and

(4) continues in full force and effect, without resorting to strike or lockout, all the terms and conditions of the existing contract for a period of sixty days after such notice is given or until the expiration date of such contract, whichever occurs later:

The duties imposed upon employers, employees, and labor organi - zations by paragraphs (2), (3), and (4) shall becom inapplicable upon an intervening certification of the Board, under which the labor organization or individual, which is a party to the contract, has been superseded as or ceased to be the representative of the employees subject to the provisions of section 9(a), and the duties so imposed shall not be construed as requiring either party to dis - cuss or agree to any modification of the terms and conditions contained in a contract for a fixed period, if such modification is to become effective before such terms and conditions can be reopened under the provisions of the contract. Any employee who engages in a strike within the sixty-day period specified in this subsection shall lose his status as an employee of the employer engaged in the particular labor dispute, for the purposes of section 8, 9, and 10 of this Act, as amended, but such loss of status for such employee shall terminate if and when he is reemployed by such employer.

Appendix I

EXECUTIVE ORDER 10988
EMPLOYEE-MANAGEMENT COOPERATION
IN THE FEDERAL SERVICE

WHEREAS participation of employees in the formulation and
implementation of personnel policies affecting them contributes
to effective conduct of public business; and

WHEREAS the efficient administration of the Government
and the well-being of employees require that orderly and constructive relationships be maintained between employee organizations and management officials; and

WHEREAS subject to law the paramount requirements of the
public service, employee-management relations within the Federal service should be improved by providing employees an opportunity for greater participation in the formulation and implementation of policies and procedures affecting the conditions of
their employment; and

WHEREAS effective employee-management cooperation in
the public service requires a clear statement of the respective
rights and obligations of employee organizations and agency management:

NOW, THEREFORE, by virtue of the authority vested in me
by the Constitution of the United States, by section 1753 of the
Revised Statutes (5 U.S.C. 631), and as President of the United
States, I hereby direct that the following policies shall govern
officers and agencies of the executive branch of the Government
in all dealings with Federal employees and organizations representing such employees.

Section 1. (a) Employees of the Federal Government shall
have, and shall be protected in the exercise of, the right, freely
and without fear of penalty or reprisal, to form, join and assist
any employee organization or to refrain from any such activity.
Except as hereinafter expressly provided, the freedom of such

161

employees to assist any employee organization shall be recognized as extending to participation in the management of the organization and acting for the organization in the capacity of an organization representative, including presentation of its views to officials of the executive branch, the Congress or other appropriate authority. The head of each executive department and agency (hereinafter referred to as "agency") shall take such action, consistent with law, as may be required in order to assure that employees in the agency are apprised of the rights described in this section, and that no interference, restraint, coercion or discrimination is practiced within such agency to encourage or discourage membership in any employee organization.

(b) The rights described in this section do not extend to participation in the management of an employee organization, or acting as a representative of any such organization, where such participation or activity would result in a conflict of interest or otherwise be incompatible with law or with the official duties of an employee.

Section 2.   When used in this order, the term "employee organization" means any lawful association, labor organization, federation, council, or brotherhood having as a primary purpose the improvement of working conditions among Federal employees, or any craft, trade, or industrial union whose membership includes both Federal employees and employees of private organizations; but such term shall not include any organization (1) which asserts the right to strike against the Government of the United States or any agency thereof, or to assist or participate in any such strike, or which imposes a duty or obligation to conduct, assist or participate in any such strike, or (2) which advocates the overthrow of the constitutional form of Government in the United States, or (3) which discriminates with regard to the terms or conditions of membership because of race, color, creed or national origin.

Section 3.   (a) Agencies shall accord informal, formal or exclusive recognition to employee organizations which requests such recognition in conformity with the requirements specified in sections 4, 5 and 6 of this order, except that no recognition shall be accorded to any employee organization which the head of the agency considers to be so subject to corrupt influences or influences opposed to basic democratic principles that recognition would be inconsistent with the objectives of this order.

(b) Recognition of an employee organization shall continue so long as such organization satisfies the criteria of this order applicable to such recognition; but nothing in this section shall require any agency to determine whether an organization should become or continue to be recognized as exclusive representative of the employees in any unit within 12 months after a prior determination of exclusive status with respect to such unit has been made pursuant to the provisions of this order.

(c) Recognition, in whatever form accorded, shall not--

(1) preclude any employee, regardless of employee organization membership, from bringing matters of personal concern to the attention of appropriate officials in accordance with applicable law, rule, regulation, or established agency policy, or from choosing his own representative in a grievance or appellate action; or

(2) preclude or restrict consultations and dealings between an agency and any veterans organization with respect to matters of particular interest to employees with veterans preference; or

(3) preclude an agency from consulting or dealing with any religious, social, fraternal or other lawful association, not qualified as an employee organization, with respect to matters or policies which involve individual members of the association or are of particular applicability to it or its members, when such consultations or dealings are duly limited so as not to assume the character of formal consultation on matters of general employee-management policy or to extend to areas where recognition of the interests of one employee group may result in discrimination against or injury to the interests of other employees.

Section 4. (a) An agency shall accord an employee organization, which does not qualify for exclusive or formal recognition, informal recognition as representative of its member employees without regard to whether any other employee organization has been accorded formal or exclusive recognition as representative of some or all employees in any unit.

(b) When an employee organization has been informally recognized, it shall, to the extent consistent with the efficient and orderly conduct of the public business, be permitted to present to appropriate officials its views on matters of concern to its members. The agency need not, however, consult with an employee organization so recognized in the formulation of personnel or other policies with respect to such matters.

Section 5. (a) An agency shall accord an employee organization formal recognition as the representative of its members in a unit as defined by the agency when (1) no other employee organization is qualified for exclusive recognition as representative of employees in the unit, (2) it is determined by the agency that the employee organization has a substantial and stable membership of no less than 10 per centum of the employees in the unit, and (3) the employee organization has submitted to the agency a roster of its officers and representatives, a copy of its constitution and by-laws, and a statement of objectives. When, in the opinion of the head of an agency, an employee organization has a sufficient number of local organizations or a sufficient total membership within such agency, such organization may be accorded formal recognition at the national level with any other employee organization on matters affecting its members.

(b) When an employee organization has been formally recognized, the agency, through appropriate officials, shall consult with such organization from time to time in the formulation and implementation of personnel policies and practices, and matters affecting working conditions that are of concern to its members. Any such organization shall be entitled from time to time to raise such matters for discussion with appropriate officials and at all times to present its views thereon in writing. In no case, however, shall an agency be required to consult with an employee organization which has been formally recognized with respect to any matter which, if the employee organization were one entitled to exclusive recognition, would not be included within the obligation to meet and confer, as described in section 6(b) of this order.

Section 6. (a) An agency shall recognize an employee organization as the exclusive representative of the employees in an appropriate unit when such organization is eligible for formal recognition pursuant to section 5 of this order, and has been designated or selected by a majority of the employees of such unit as the representative of such employees in such unit. Units may be established on any plant or installation, craft, functional or other basis which will ensure a clear and identifiable community of interest among the employees concerned, but no unit shall be established solely on the basis of the extent to which employees in the proposed unit have organized. Except where otherwise required by established practice, prior agreement, or special circumstances, no unit shall be established for purposes of exclusive recognition which includes (1) any managerial executive, (2) any employee engaged in Federal personnel work in other than a purely clerical capacity, (3) both supervisors who officially evaluate the performance of employees and the employees whom they supervise, or (4) both professional employees and nonprofessional employees unless a majority of such professional employees vote for inclusion in such unit.

(b) When an employee organization has been recognized as the exclusive representative of employees of an appropriate unit it shall be entitled to act for and to negotiate agreements covering all employees in the unit and shall be responsible for representing the interests of all such employees without discrimination and without regard to employee organization membership. Such employee organization shall be given the opportunity to be represented at discussions between management and employees or employee representatives concerning grievances, personnel policies and practices, or other matters affecting general working conditions of employees in the unit. The agency and such employee organization, through appropriate officials and representatives, shall meet at reasonable times and confer with respect to personnel policy and practices and matters affecting working conditions, so far as may be appropriate subjects to law and policy requirements. This extends to the negotiation of an agreement, or any question arising thereunder, the determination of appropriate techniques, consistent with the terms and purposes of this order, to assist in such negotiation, and the execution of a written memorandum of agreement or understanding incorporating any agreement reached by the parties. In exercising authority to make rules and regulations relating to personnel policies and practices and working conditions, agencies shall have due regard for the obligation imposed by this section, but such obligation shall not be construed to extend to such areas of discretion and policy as the mission of an agency, its budget, its organization and the assignment of its personnel, or the technology of performing its work.

Section 7. Any basic or initial agreement entered into with an employee organization as the exclusive representative of employees in a unit must be approved by the head of the agency or any official designated by him. All agreements with such employee organizations shall also be subject to the following requirements, which shall be expressly stated in the initial or basic agreement and shall be applicable to all supplemental, implementing, subsidiary or informal agreements between the agency and the organization.

(1) In the administration of all matters covered by the agreement officials and employees are governed by the provisions of any existing or future laws and regulations, including policies set forth in the Federal Personnel Manual and agency regulations, which may be applicable, and the agreement shall at all times be applied subject to such laws, regulations and policies;

(2) Management officials of the agency retain the right, in accordance with applicable laws and regulations, (a) to direct employees of the agency, (b) to hire, promote, transfer, assign, and retain employees in positions within the agency, and to suspend, demote, discharge, or take other disciplinary action against employees, (c) to relieve employees from duties because of lack of work or for other legitimate reasons, (d) to maintain the efficiency of the Government operations entrusted to them, (e) to determine the methods, means and personnel by which such operations are to be conducted; and (f) to take whatever actions may be necessary to carry out the mission of the agency in situations of emergency.

Section 8. (a) Agreements entered into or negotiated in accordance with this order with an employee organization which is the exclusive representative of employees in an appropriate unit may contain provisions, applicable only to employees in the unit, concerning procedures for consideration of grievances. Such procedures (1) shall conform to standards issued by the Civil Service Commission, and (2) may not in any manner diminish or impair any rights which would otherwise be available to any employee in the absence of an agreement providing for such procedures.

166

(b) Procedures established by an agreement which are otherwise in conformity with this section may include provisions for the arbitration of grievances. Such arbitration (1) shall be advisory in nature with any decisions or recommendations subject to the approval of the agency head; (2) shall extend only to the interpretation or application of agreements or agency policy and not to changes in or proposed changes in agreements or agency policy; and (3) shall be invoked only with the approval of the individual employee or employees concerned.

Section 9. Solicitation of memberships, dues, or other internal employee organization business shall be conducted during the non-duty hours of the employees concerned. Officially requested or approved consultations and meetings between management officials and representatives of recognized employee organizations shall, wherever practicable, be conducted on official time, but any agency may require that negotiations with an employee organization which has been accorded exclusive recognition be conducted during the non-duty hours of the employee organization representatives involved in such negotiations.

Section 10. No later than July 1, 1962, the head of each agency shall issue appropriate policies, rules and regulations for the implementation of this order, including: A clear statement of the rights of its employees under the order; policies and procedures with respect to recognition of employee organizations; procedures for determining appropriate employee units; policies and practices regarding consultation with representatives of employee organizations, other organizations and individual employees; and policies with respect to the use of agency facilities by employee organizations. Insofar as may be practicable and appropriate, agencies shall consult with representatives of employee organizations in the formulation of these policies, rules and regulations.

Section 11. Each agency shall be responsible for determining in accordance with this order whether a unit is appropriate for purposes of exclusive recognition and, by an election or other appropriate means, whether an employee organization represents a majority of the employees in such a unit so as to be entitled to such recognition. Upon the request of any agency, or of any employee organization which is seeking exclusive recognition and which qualifies for or has been accorded formal recognition, the Secretary of Labor, subject to such necessary rules as he may prescribe, shall nominate from the National Panel of Arbitrators maintained by the Federal Mediation and Conciliation Service one or more qualified arbitrators who will be available for employment by the agency concerned for either or both of the following purposes, as may be required: (1) to investigate the facts and issue an advisory decision as to the appropriateness of a unit for purposes of exclusive recognition and as to related issues submitted for consideration; (2) to conduct or supervise an election or otherwise determine by such means as may be appropriate, and on an advisory basis, whether an employee organization represents the majority of the employees in a unit. Consonant with law, the Secretary of Labor shall render such assistance as may be appropriate in connection with advisory decisions or determinations under this section, but the necessary costs of such assistance shall be paid by the agency to which it relates. In the event questions as to the appropriateness of a unit or the majority status of an employee organization shall arise in the Department of Labor, the duties described in this section which would otherwise be the responsibility of the Secretary of Labor shall be performed by the Civil Service Commission.

Section 12. The Civil Service Commission shall establish and maintain a program to assist in carrying out the objectives of this order. The Commission shall develop a program for the guidance of agencies in employee-management relations in the Federal service; provide technical advice to the agencies on employee-management programs; assist in the development of programs for training agency personnel in the principles and procedures of consultation, negotiation and the settlement of disputes in the Federal service, and for the training of management officials in the discharge of their employee-management relations responsibilities in the public interest; provide for continuous study and review of the Federal employee-management relations program and, from time to time, make recommendations to the President for its improvement.

Section 13. (a) The Civil Service Commission and the Department of Labor shall jointly prepare (1) proposed standards of conduct for employee organizations and (2) a proposed code of fair labor practices in employee-management relations in the Federal service appropriate to assist in securing the uniform and effective implementation of the policies, rights and responsibilities described in this order.

(b) There is hereby established the President's Temporary Committee on the Implementation of the Federal Employee-Management Relations Program. The Committee shall consist of the Secretary of Labor, who shall be chairman of the Committee, the Secretary of Defense, the Postmaster General, and the Chairman of the Civil Service Commission. In addition to such other matters relating to the implementation of this order as may be referred to it by the President, the Committee shall advise the President with respect to any problems arising out of completion of agreements pursuant to sections 6 and 7, and shall receive the proposed standards of conduct for employee organizations and proposed code of fair labor practices in the Federal service, as described in this section, and report thereon to the President with such recommendations or amendments as it may deem appropriate. Consonant with law, the departments and agencies represented on the Committee shall, as may be necessary for the effectuation of this section, furnish assistance to the Committee in accordance with section 214 of the Act of May 3, 1945, 59 Stat. 134 (31 U.S.C. 691). Unless otherwise directed by the President, the Committee shall cease to exist 30 days after the date on which it submits its report to the President pursuant to this section.

Section 14. The head of each agency, in accordance with the provisions of this order and regulations prescribed by the Civil Service Commission, shall extend to all employees in the competitive civil service rights identical in adverse action cases to those provided preference eligibles under section 14 of the Veterans' Preference Act of 1944, as amended. Each employee in the competitive service shall have the right to appeal to the Civil Service Commission from an adverse decision of the administrative officer so acting, such appeal to be processed in an identical manner to that provided for appeals under section 14 of the Veterans' Preference Act. Any recommendation by the Civil Service

Commission submitted to the head of an agency on the basis of an appeal by an employee in the competitive service shall be complied with by the head of the agency. This section shall become effective as to all adverse actions commenced by issuance of a notification of proposed action on or after July 1, 1962.

Section 15. Nothing in this order shall be construed to annul or modify, or to preclude the renewal or continuation of, any lawful agreement heretofore entered into between any agency and any representative of its employees or other organization prior to the time that the status and representation rights of such representative or organization are determined in conformity with this order.

Section 16. This order (except section 14) shall not apply to the Federal Bureau of Investigation, the Central Intelligence Agency, or any other agency, or to any office, bureau or entity within an agency, primarily performing intelligence, investigation, or security functions if the head of the agency determines that the provisions of this order cannot be applied in a manner consistent with national security requirements and considerations. When he deems it necessary in the national interest, and subject to such conditions as he may prescribe, the head of any agency may suspend any provision of this order (except section 14) with respect to any agency installation or activity which is located outside of the United States.

JOHN F. KENNEDY

THE WHITE HOUSE

No. 10988

January 17, 1962

USCSC--WASHINGTON D C

Appendix J

LABOR-MANAGEMENT RELATIONS
IN THE FEDERAL SERVICE

WHEREAS the public interest requires high standards of employee performance and the continual development and implementation of modern and progressive work practices to facilitate ' improved employee performance and efficiency; and

WHEREAS the well-being of employees and efficient administration of the Government are benefited by providing employees an opportunity to participate in the formulation and implementation of personnel policies and practices affecting the conditions of their employment; and

WHEREAS the participation of employees should be improved through the maintenance of constructive and cooperative relationships between labor organizations and management officials; and

WHEREAS subject to law and the paramount requirements of public service, effective labor-management relations within the Federal service require a clear statement of the respective rights and obligations of labor organizations and agency management:

NOW, THEREFORE, by virtue of the authority vested in me by the Constitution and statutes of the United States, including sections 3301 and 7301 of title 5 of the United States Code, and as President of the United States, I hereby direct that the following policies shall govern officers and agencies of the executive branch of the Government in all dealings with Federal employees and organizations representing such employees.

GENERAL PROVISIONS

Section 1. Policy. (a) Each employee of the executive branch of the Federal Government has the right, freely and without fear of penalty or reprisal, to form, join, and assist a labor organization or to refrain from any such activity, and each employee shall be protected in the exercise of this right. Except as otherwise expressly provided in this Order, the right to assist a labor organization extends to participation in the management of the organization and acting for the organization in the capacity of an organization representative, including presentation of its views to officials of the executive branch, the Congress, or other appropriate authority. The head of each agency shall take the action required to assure that employees in the agency are apprised of their rights under this section, and that no interference, restraint, coercion, or discrimination is practiced within his agency to encourage or discourage membership in a labor organization.

(b) Paragraph (a) of this section does not authorize participation in the management of a labor organization or acting as a representative of such an organization by a supervisor, except as provided in section 24 of this Order, or by an employee when the participation or activity would result in a conflict or apparent conflict of interest or otherwise be incompatible with law or with the official duties of the employee.

Sec. 2. Definitions. When used in this Order, the term —

(a) "Agency" means an executive department, a Government corporation, and an independent establishment as defined in section 104 of title 5, United States Code, except the General Accounting Office;

(b) "Employee" means an employee of an agency and an employee of a nonappropriated fund instrumentality of the United States but does not include, for the purpose of formal or exclusive recognition or national consultation rights, a supervisor, except as provided in section 24 of this order;

(c) "Supervisor" means an employee having authority, in the interest of an agency, to hire, transfer, suspend, lay off, recall, promote, discharge, assign, reward, or discipline other employees, or responsibly to direct them, or to evaluate their performance, or to adjust their grievances, or effectively to recommend such action, if in connection with the foregoing the exercise of authority is not of a merely routine or clerical nature, but requires the use of independent judgment;

(d) "Guard" means an employee assigned to enforce against employees and other persons rules to protect agency property or the safety of persons on agency premises, or to maintain law and order in areas or facilities under Government control;

(e) "Labor organization" means a lawful organization of any kind in which employees participate and which exists for the purpose, in whole or in part, of dealing with agencies concerning grievances, personnel policies and practices, or other matters affecting the working conditions of their employees; but does not include an organization which --

(1) consists of management officials or supervisors, except as provided in section 24 of this Order;

(2) asserts the right to strike against the Government of the United States or any agency thereof, or to assist or participate in such a strike, or imposes a duty or obligation to conduct, assist or participate in such a strike;

(3) advocates the overthrow of the constitutional form of government in the United States; or

(4) discriminates with regard to the terms or conditions of membership because of race, color, creed, sex, age, or national origin;

(f) "Agency management" means the agency head and all management officials, supervisors, and other representatives of management having authority to act for the agency on any matters relating to the implementation of the agency labor-management relations program established under this Order;

(g) "Council" means the Federal Labor Relations Council established by this Order;

(h) "Panel" means the Federal Service Impasses Panel established by this Order; and

(i) "Assistant Secretary" means the Assistant Secretary of Labor for Labor-Management Relations.

Sec. 3. Application. (a) This Order applies to all employees and agencies in the executive branch, except as provided in paragraphs (b), (c) and (d) of this section.

(b) This Order (except section 22) does not apply to --

(1) the Federal Bureau of Investigation;

(2) the Central Intelligence Agency;

(3) any other agency, or office, bureau, or entity within an agency, which has as a primary function intelligence, investigative, or security work, when the head of the agency determines, in his sole judgment, that the Order cannot be applied in a manner consistent with national security requirements and considerations; or

(4) any office, bureau or entity within an agency which has as a primary function investigation or audit of the conduct or work of officials or employees of the agency for the purpose of ensuring honesty and integrity in the discharge of their official duties, when the head of the agency determines, in his sole judgment, that the Order cannot be applied in a manner consistent with the internal security of the agency.

(c) The head of an agency may, in his sole judgment, suspend any provision of this Order (except section 22) with respect to any agency installation or activity located outside the United States, when he determines that this is necessary in the national interest, subject to the conditions he prescribes.

(d) Employees engaged in administering a labor-management relations law or this Order shall not be represented by a labor organization which also represents other groups of employees under the law or this Order, or which is affiliated directly or indirectly with an organization which represents such a group of employees.

ADMINISTRATION

Sec. 4. <u>Federal Labor Relations Council</u>. (a) There is hereby established the Federal Labor Relations Council, which consists of the Chairman of the Civil Service Commission, who shall be chairman of the Council, the Secretary of Labor, an official of the Executive Office of the President, and such other officials of the executive branch as the President may designate from time to time. The Civil Service Commission shall provide services and staff assistance to the Council to the extent authorized by law.

(b) The Council shall administer and interpret this Order, decide major policy issues, prescribe regulations, and from time to time, report and make recommendations to the President.

(c) The Council may consider, subject to its regulations --

(1) appeals from decisions of the Assistant Secretary issued pursuant to section 6 of this Order;

(2) appeals on negotiability issues as provided in section 11 (c) of this Order;

(3) exceptions to arbitration awards; and

(4) other matters it deems appropriate to assure the effectuation of the purposes of this Order.

Sec. 5. <u>Federal Service Impasses Panel</u>. (a) There is hereby established the Federal Service Impasses Panel as an agency within the Council. The Panel consists of at least three members appointed by the President, one of whom he designates as chairman. The Council shall provide the services and staff assistance needed by the Panel.

(b) The Panel may consider negotiation impasses as provided in section 17 of this Order and may take any action it considers necessary to settle an impasse.

(c) The Panel shall prescribe regulations needed to administer its function under this Order.

Sec. 6. <u>Assistant Secretary of Labor for Labor-Management Relations</u>. (a) The Assistant Secretary shall --

(1) decide questions as to the appropriate unit for the purpose of exclusive recognition and related issues submitted for his consideration;

(2) supervise elections to determine whether a labor organization is the choice of a majority of the employees in an appropriate unit as their exclusive representative, and certify the results;

(3) decide questions as to the eligibility of labor organizations for national consultation rights under criteria prescribed by the Council; and

(4) except as provided in section 19 (d) of this Order, decide complaints of alleged unfair labor practices and alleged violations of the standards of conduct for labor organizations.

(b) In any matters arising under paragraph (a) of this section, the Assistant Secretary may require an agency or a labor organization to cease and desist from violations of this Order and require it to take such affirmative action as he considers appropriate to effectuate the policies of this Order.

(c) In performing the duties imposed on him by this section, the Assistant Secretary may request and use the services and assistance of employees of other agencies in accordance with. section 1 of the Act of March 4, 1915, (38 Stat. 1084, as amended; 31 U.S.C. §686).

(d) The Assistant Secretary shall prescribe regulations needed to administer his functions under this Order.

(e) If any matters arising under paragraph (a) of this section involve the Department of Labor, the duties of the Assistant Secretary described in paragraphs (a) and (b) of this section shall be performed by a member of the Civil Service Commission designated by the Chairman of the Commission.

Sec. 7. <u>Recognition in general</u>. (a) An agency shall accord exclusive recognition or national consultation rights at the request of a labor organization which meets the requirements for the recognition or consultation rights under this Order.

(b) A labor organization seeking recognition shall submit to the agency a roster of its officers and representatives, a copy of its constitution and by-laws, and a statement of its objectives.

(c) When recognition of a labor organization has been accorded, the recognition continues as long as the organization continues to meet the requirements of this Order applicable to that recognition, except that this section does not require an election to determine whether an organization should become, or continue to be recognized as, exclusive representative of the employees in any unit or subdivision thereof within 12 months after a prior valid election with respect to such unit.

(d) Recognition, in whatever form accorded, does not --

(1) preclude an employee, regardless of whether he is a member of a labor organization, from bringing matters of personal concern to the attention of appropriate officials under applicable law, rule, regulations, or established agency policy; or from choosing his own representative in a grievance or appellate action;

(2) preclude or restrict consultations and dealings between an agency and a veterans organization with respect to matters of particular interest to employees with veterans preference; or

(3) preclude an agency from consulting or dealing with a religious, social, fraternal, or other lawful association, not qualified as a labor organization, with respect to matters or policies which involve individual members of the association or are of particular applicability to it or its members.
Consultations and dealings under subparagraph (3) of this paragraph shall be so limited that they do not assume the character of formal consultation on matters of general employee-management policy, except as provided in paragraph (e) of this section, or extend to areas where recognition of the interests of one employee group may result in discrimination against or injury to the interests of other employees.

(e) An agency shall establish a system for intra-management communication and consultation with its supervisors or associations of supervisors. The communications and consultations shall have as their purposes the improvement of agency operations, the improvement of working conditions of supervisors, the exchange of information, the improvement of managerial effectiveness, and the establishment of policies that best serve the public interest in accomplishing the mission of the agency.

(f) Informal recognition shall not be accorded after the date of this Order.

Sec. 8 <u>Formal Recognition.</u> (a) Formal recognition, including formal recognition at the national level, shall not be accorded after the date of this Order.

(b) An agency shall continue any formal recognition, including formal recognition at the national level, accorded a labor organization before the date of this Order until --

(1) the labor organization ceases to be eligible under this Order for formal recognition so accorded;

(2) a labor organization is accorded exclusive recognition as representative of employees in the unit to which the formal recognition applies; or

(3) the formal recognition is terminated under regulations prescribed by the Federal Labor Relations Council.

(c) When a labor organization holds formal recognition, it is the representative of its members in a unit as defined by the agency when recognition was accorded. The agency, through appropriate officials, shall consult with representatives of the organization from time to time in the formulation and implementation of personnel policies and practices, and matters affecting working conditions that affect members of the organization in the unit to which the formal recognition applies. The organization is entitled from time to time to raise such matters for discussion with appropriate officials and at all times to present its views thereon in writing. The agency is not required to consult with the labor organization on any matter on which it would not be required to meet and confer if the labor organization were entitled to exclusive recognition.

Sec. 9. _National consultation rights._ (a) An agency shall accord national consultation rights to a labor organization which qualifies under criteria established by the Federal Labor Relations Council as the representative of a substantial number of employees of the agency. National consultation rights shall not be accorded for any unit where a labor organization already holds exclusive recognition at the national level for that unit. The granting of national consultation rights does not preclude an agency from appropriate dealings at the national level with other organizations on matters affecting their members. An agency shall terminate national consultation rights when the labor organization ceases to qualify under the established criteria.

(b) When a labor organization has been accorded national consultation rights, thé agency, through appropriate officials, shall notify representatives of the organization of proposed substantive changes in personnel policies that affect employees it represents and provide an opportunity for the organization to comment on the proposed changes. The labor organization may suggest changes in the agency's personnel policies and have its views carefully considered. It may confer in person at reasonable times, on request, with appropriate officials on personnel policy matters, and at all times present its views thereon in writing. An agency is not required to consult with a labor organization on any matter on which it would not be required to meet and confer if the organization were entitled to exclusive recognition.

(c) Questions as to the eligibility of labor organizations for national consultation rights may be referred to the Assistant Secretary for decision.

Sec. 10. _Exclusive recognition._ (a) An agency shall accord exclusive recognition to a labor organization when the organization has been selected, in a secret ballot election, by a majority of the employees in an appropriate unit as their representative.

(b) A unit may be established on a plant or installation, craft, functional, or other basis which will ensure a clear and identifiable community of interest among the employees concerned and will promote effective dealings and efficiency of agency operations. A unit shall not be established solely on the basis of the extent to which employees in the proposed unit have organized, nor shall a unit be established if it includes --

(1) any management official or supervisor, except as provided in section 24;

(2) an employee engaged in Federal personnel work in other than a purely clerical capacity;

(3) any guard together with other employees; or

(4) both professional and nonprofessional employees, unless a majority of the professional employees vote for inclusion in the unit.
Questions as to the appropriate unit and related issues may be referred to the Assistant Secretary for decision.

(c) An agency shall not accord exclusive recognition to a labor organization as the representative of employees in a unit of guards if the organization admits to membership, or is affiliated directly or indirectly with an organization which admits to membership, employees other than guards.

(d) All elections shall be conducted under the supervision of the Assistant Secretary, or persons designated by him, and shall be by secret ballot. Each employee eligible to vote shall be provided the opportunity to choose the labor organization he wishes to represent him, from among those on the ballot, or "no union." Elections may be held to determine whether --

(1) a labor organization should be recognized as the exclusive representative of employees in a unit;

(2) a labor organization should replace another labor organization as the exclusive representative; or

(3) a labor organization should cease to be the exclusive representative.

(e) When a labor organization has been accorded exclusive recognition, it is the exclusive representative of employees in the unit and is entitled to act for and to negotiate agreements covering all employees in the unit. It is responsible for representing the interests of all employees in the unit without discrimination and without regard to labor organization membership. The labor organization shall be given the opportunity to be represented at formal discussions between management and employees or employee representatives concerning grievances, personnel policies and practices, or other matters affecting general working conditions of employees in the unit.

AGREEMENTS

Sec. 11. Negotiation of agreements. (a) An agency and a labor organization that has been accorded exclusive recognition, through appropriate representatives, shall meet at reasonable times and confer in good faith with respect to personnel policies and practices and matters affecting working conditions, so far as may be appropriate under applicable laws and regulations, including policies set forth in the Federal Personnel Manual, published agency policies and regulations, a national or other controlling agreement at a higher level in the agency, and this Order. They may negotiate an agreement, or any question arising thereunder; determine appropriate techniques, consistent with section 17 of this Order, to assist in such negotiation; and execute a written agreement or memorandum of understanding.

(b) In prescribing regulations relating to personnel policies and practices and working conditions, an agency shall have due regard for the obligation imposed by paragraph (a) of this section. However, the obligation to meet and confer does not include matters with respect to the mission of an agency; its budget; its organization; the number of employees; and the numbers, types, and grades of positions or employees assigned to an organizational unit, work project or tour of duty; the technology of performing its work; or its internal security practices. This does not preclude the parties from negotiating agreements providing appropriate arrangements for employees adversely affected by the impact of realignment of work forces or technological change.

(c) If, in connection with negotiations, an issue develops as to whether a proposal is contrary to law, regulation, controlling agreement, or this Order and therefore not negotiable, it shall be resolved as follows:

(1) An issue which involves interpretation of a controlling agreement at a higher agency level is resolved under the procedures of the controlling agreement, or, if none, under agency regulations;

(2) An issue other than as described in subparagraph (1) of this paragraph which arises at a local level may be referred by either party to the head of the agency for determination;

(3) An agency head's determination as to the interpretation of the agency's regulations with respect to a proposal is final;

(4) A labor organization may appeal to the Council for a decision when --

(i) it disagrees with an agency head's determination that a proposal would violate applicable law, regulation of appropriate authority outside the agency, or this Order, or

(ii) it believes that an agency's regulations, as interpreted by the agency head, violate applicable law, regulation of appropriate authority outside the agency, or this Order.

Sec. 12. Basic provisions of agreements. Each agreement between an agency and a labor organization is subject to the following requirements --

(a) in the administration of all matters covered by the agreement, officials and employees are governed by existing or future laws and the regulations of appropriate authorities, including policies set forth in the Federal Personnel Manual; by published agency policies and regulations in existence at the time the agreement was approved; and by subsequently published agency policies and regulations required by law or by the regulations of appropriate authorities, or authorized by the terms of a controlling agreement at a higher agency level;

(b) management officials of the agency retain the right, in accordance with applicable laws and regulations --

(1) to direct employees of the agency;

(2) to hire, promote, transfer, assign, and retain employees in positions within the agency, and to suspend, demote, discharge, or take other disciplinary action against employees;

(3) to relieve employees from duties because of lack of work or for other legitimate reasons;

(4) to maintain the efficiency of the Government operations entrusted to them;

(5) to determine the methods, means, and personnel by which such operations are to be conducted; and

(6) to take whatever actions may be necessary to carry out the mission of the agency in situations of emergency; and

(c) nothing in the agreement shall require an employee to become or to remain a member of a labor organization, or to pay money to the organization except pursuant to a voluntary, written authorization by a member for the payment of dues through payroll deductions.
The requirements of this section shall be expressly stated in the initial or basic agreement and apply to all supplemental, implementing, subsidiary, or informal agreements between the agency and the organization.

Sec. 13. Grievance procedures. An agreement with a labor organization which is the exclusive representative of employees in an appropriate unit may provide procedures, applicable only to employees in the unit, for the consideration of employee grievances and of disputes over the interpretation and application of agreements. The procedure for consideration of employee grievances shall meet the requirements for negotiated grievance procedures established by the Civil Service Commission. A negotiated employee grievance procedure which conforms to this section, to applicable laws, and to regulations of the Civil Service Commission and the agency is the exclusive procedure available to employees in the unit when the agreement so provides.

Sec. 14. Arbitration of grievances. (a) Negotiated procedures may provide for the arbitration of employee grievances and of disputes over the interpretation or application of existing agreements. Negotiated procedures may not extend arbitration to changes or proposed changes in agreements or agency policy. Such procedures shall provide for the invoking of arbitration only with the approval of the labor organization that has exclusive recognition and, in the case of an employee grievance, only with the approval of the employee. The costs of the arbitrator shall be shared equally by the parties.

(b) Either party may file exceptions to an arbitrator's award with the Council, under regulations prescribed by the Council.

Sec. 15. Approval of agreements. An agreement with a labor organization as the exclusive representative of employees in a unit is subject to the approval of the head of the agency or an official designated by him. An agreement shall be approved if it conforms to applicable laws, existing published agency policies and regulations (unless the agency has granted an exception to a policy or regulation) and regulations of other appropriate authorities. A local agreement subject to a national or other controlling agreement at a higher level shall be approved under the procedures of the controlling agreement, or, if none, under agency regulations.

NEGOTIATION DISPUTES AND IMPASSES

Sec. 16. Negotiation disputes. The Federal Mediation and Conciliation Service shall provide services and assistance to Federal agencies and labor organizations in the resolution of negotiation disputes. The Service shall determine under what circumstances and in what manner it shall proffer its services.

Sec. 17. Negotiation impasses. When voluntary arrangements, including the services of the Federal Mediation and Conciliation Service or other third-party mediation, fail to resolve a negotiation impasse, either party may request the Federal Service Impasses Panel to consider the matter. The Panel, in its discretion and under the regulations it prescribes, may consider the matter and may recommend procedures to the parties for the resolution of the impasse or may settle the impasse by appropriate action. Arbitration or third-party fact finding with recommendations to assist in the resolution of an impasse may be used by the parties only when authorized or directed by the Panel.

CONDUCT OF LABOR ORGANIZATIONS AND MANAGEMENT

Sec. 18. Standards of conduct for labor organizations.

(a) An agency shall accord recognition only to a labor organization that is free from corrupt influences and influences opposed to basic democratic principles. Except as provided in paragraph (b) of this section, an organization is not required to prove that it has the required freedom when it is subject to governing requirements adopted by the organization or by a national or international labor organization or federation of labor organizations with which it is affiliated or in which it participates, containing explicit and detailed provisions to which it subscribes calling for --

(1) the maintenance of democratic procedures and practices, including provisions for periodic elections to be conducted subject to recognized safeguards and provisions defining and securing the right of individual members to participation in the affairs of the organization, to fair and equal treatment under the governing rules of the organization, and to fair process in disciplinary proceedings;

(2) the exclusion from office in the organization of persons affiliated with Communist or other totalitarian movements and persons identified with corrupt influences;

(3) the prohibition of business or financial interests on the part of organization officers and agents which conflict with their duty to the organization and its members; and

(4) the maintenance of fiscal integrity in the conduct of the affairs of the organization, including provision for accounting and financial controls and regular financial reports or summaries to be made available to members.

(b) Notwithstanding the fact that a labor organization has adopted or subscribed to standards of conduct as provided in paragraph (a) of this section, the organization is required to furnish evidence of its freedom from corrupt influences or influences opposed to basic democratic principles when there is reasonable cause to believe that --

(1) the organization has been suspended or expelled from or is subject to other sanction by a parent labor organization or federation of organizations with which it had been affiliated because it has demonstrated an unwillingness or inability to comply with governing requirements comparable in purpose to those required by paragraph (a) of this section; or

(2) the organization is in fact subject to influences that would preclude recognition under this Order.

(c) A labor organization which has or seeks recognition as a representative of employees under this Order shall file financial and other reports, provide for bonding of officials and employees of the organization, and comply with trusteeship and election standards.

(d) The Assistant Secretary shall prescribe the regulations needed to effectuate this section. These regulations shall conform generally to the principles applied to unions in the private sector. Complaints of violations of this section shall be filed with the Assistant Secretary.

Sec. 19. Unfair labor practices. (a) Agency management shall not --

(1) interfere with, restrain, or coerce an employee in the exercise of the rights assured by this Order;

(2) encourage or discourage membership in a labor organization by discrimination in regard to hiring, tenure, promotion, or other conditions of employment;

(3) sponsor, control, or otherwise assist a labor organization, except that an agency may furnish customary and routine services and facilities under section 23 of this Order when consistent with the best interests of the agency, its employees, and the organization, and when the services and facilities are furnished, if requested, on an impartial basis to organizations having equivalent status;

(4) discipline or otherwise discriminate against an employee because he has filed a complaint or given testimony under this Order;

(5) refuse to accord appropriate recognition to a labor organization qualified for such recognition; or

(6) refuse to consult, confer, or negotiate with a labor organization as required by this Order.

(b) A labor organization shall not --

(1) interfere with, restrain, or coerce an employee in the exercise of his rights assured by this Order;

(2) attempt to induce agency management to coerce an employee in the exercise of his rights under this Order;

(3) coerce, attempt to coerce, or discipline, fine, or take other economic sanction against a member of the organization as punishment or reprisal for, or for the purpose of hindering or impeding his work performance, his productivity, or the discharge of his duties owed as an officer or employee of the United States;

(4) call or engage in a strike, work stoppage, or slowdown; picket an agency in a labor-management dispute; or condone any such activity by failing to take affirmative action to prevent or stop it;

(5) discriminate against an employee with regard to the terms or conditions of membership because of race, color, creed, sex, age, or national origin; or

(6) refuse to consult, confer, or negotiate with an agency as required by this Order.

(c) A labor organization which is accorded exclusive recognition shall not deny membership to any employee in the appropriate unit except for failure to meet reasonable occupational standards uniformly required for admission, or for failure to tender initiation fees and dues uniformly required as a condition of acquiring and retaining membership. This paragraph does not preclude a labor organization from enforcing discipline in accordance with procedures under its constitution or by-laws which conform to the requirements of this Order.

(d) When the issue in a complaint of an alleged violation of paragraph (a)(1), (2), or (4) of this section is subject to an established grievance or appeals procedure, that procedure is the exclusive procedure for resolving the complaint. All other complaints of alleged violations of this section initiated by an employee, an agency, or a labor organization, that cannot be resolved by the parties, shall be filed with the Assistant Secretary.

179

MISCELLANEOUS PROVISIONS

Sec. 20. <u>Use of official time</u>. Solicitation of membership or dues, and other internal business of a labor organization, shall be conducted during the non-duty hours of the employees concerned. Employees who represent a recognized labor organization shall not be on official time when negotiating an agreement with agency management.

Sec. 21. <u>Allotment of dues</u>. (a) When a labor organization holds formal or exclusive recognition, and the agency and the organization agree in writing to this course of action, an agency may deduct the regular and periodic dues of the organization from the pay of members of the organization in the unit of recognition who make a voluntary allotment for that purpose, and shall recover the costs of making the deductions. Such an allotment is subject to the regulations of the Civil Service Commission, which shall include provision for the employee to revoke his authorization at stated six-month intervals. Such an allotment terminates when —

(1) the dues withholding agreement between the agency and the labor organization is terminated or ceases to be applicable to the employee; or

(2) the employee has been suspended or expelled from the labor organization.

(b) An agency may deduct the regular and periodic dues of an association of management officials or supervisors from the pay of members of the association who make a voluntary allotment for that purpose, and shall recover the costs of making the deductions, when the agency and the association agree in writing to this course of action. Such an allotment is subject to the regulations of the Civil Service Commission.

Sec. 22. <u>Adverse action appeals</u>. The head of each agency, in accordance with the provisions of this Order and regulations prescribed by the Civil Service Commission, shall extend to all employees in the competitive civil service rights identical in adverse action cases to those provided preference eligibles under sections 7511-7512 of title 5 of the United States Code. Each employee in the competitive service shall have the right to appeal to the Civil Service Commission from an adverse decision of the administrative officer so acting, such appeal to be processed in an identical manner to that provided for appeals under section 7701 of title 5 of the United States Code. Any recommendation by the Civil Service Commission submitted to the head of an agency on the basis of an appeal by an employee in the competitive service shall be complied with by the head of the agency.

Sec. 23. <u>Agency implementation</u>. No later than April 1, 1970, each agency shall issue appropriate policies and regulations consistent with this Order for its implementation. This includes but is not limited to a clear statement of the rights of its employees under this Order; procedures with respect to recognition of labor organizations, determination of appropriate units, consultation and negotiation with labor organizations, approval of agreements, mediation, and impasse resolution; policies with respect to the use of agency facilities by labor organizations; and policies and practices regarding consultation with other organizations and associations and individual employees. Insofar as practicable, agencies shall consult with representatives of labor organizations in the formulation of these policies and regulations, other than those for the implementation of section 7(e) of this Order.

Sec. 24. <u>Savings clauses</u>. (a) This Order does not preclude --

(1) the renewal or continuation of a lawful agreement between an agency and a representative of its employees entered into before the effective date of Executive Order No. 10988 (January 17, 1962); or

(2) the renewal, continuation, or initial according of recognition for units of management officials or supervisors represented by labor organizations which historically or traditionally represent the management officials or supervisors in private industry and which hold exclusive recognition for units of such officials or supervisors in any agency on the date of this Order.

(b) All grants of informal recognition under Executive Order No. 10988 terminate on July 1, 1970.

(c) All grants of formal recognition under Executive Order No. 10988 terminate under regulations which the Federal Labor Relations Council shall issue before October 1, 1970.

(d) By not later than December 31, 1970, all supervisors shall be excluded from units of formal and exclusive recognition and from coverage by negotiated agreements, except as provided in paragraph (a) of this section.

Sec. 25. Guidance, training, review and information.

(a) The Civil Service Commission shall establish and maintain a program for the guidance of agencies on labor-management relations in the Federal service; provide technical advice and information to agencies; assist in the development of programs for training agency personnel and management officials in labor-management relations; continuously review the operation of the Federal labor-management relations program to assist in assuring adherence to its provisions and merit system requirements; and, from time to time, report to the Council on the state of the program with any recommendations for its improvement.

(b) The Department of Labor and the Civil Service Commission shall develop programs for the collection and dissemination of information appropriate to the needs of agencies, organizations and the public.

Sec. 26. Effective date. This Order is effective on January 1, 1970 except sections 7(f) and 8 which are effective immediately. Effective January 1, 1970, Executive Order No. 10988 and the President's Memorandum of May 21, 1963, entitled Standards of Conduct for Employee Organizations and Code of Fair Labor Practices, are revoked.

RICHARD NIXON

THE WHITE HOUSE

October 29, 1969

Appendix K

FEDERAL SERVICE IMPASSES PANEL

General; Procedures of the Panel

Notice of Proposed Rule Making

Notice is hereby given that the Federal Service Impasses Panel, pursuant to section 5 of Executive Order 11491 of October 29, 1969, is considering the adoption of rules governing the organization and responsibilites of the panel. A draft of these rules is set out below as Parts 2470 and 2471, Subchapter C, Chapter XIV of Title 5 of the Code of Federal Regulations. Interested persons may submit their views and suggestions in writing to the Executive Secretary, Federal Service Impasses Panel, 1900 E. Street, N.W., Washington, D.C. 20415. All communications received within 20 days after publication of this notice in the Federal Register will be considered before the panel takes final action on the proposed rules.

PART 2470 -- GENERAL

Subpart A -- Purpose
Sec.
2470.1   Purpose.

Subpart B -- Definitions
2470.2   Definitions

AUTHORITY: The provisions of this Part 2470 issued under 5 U.S.C. 3301, 7301; Executive Order 11491, 34 F.R. 17605, 3 CFR 191, 1969 Comp.

Subpart A -- Purpose

2470.1 Purpose.

The regulations contained in this subchapter are intended to implement the provisions of sections 5 and 17 of Executive Order 11491 of October 29, 1969, entitled "Labor-Management Relations in the Federal Service." They prescribe procedures and methods which the Federal Service Impasses Panel may utilize in the resolution of negotiation impasses when the parties negotiating a labor agreement have failed to reach a full settlement by voluntary arrangements.

Subpart B -- Definitions

2470.2 Definitions.

The following definitions are used in this subchapter :
"Executive Secretary" means the Executive Secretary of the Panel.
"Factfinder(s)"means members or staff of the Panel, individuals designated by the Panel, or other persons selected jointly by the parties when so authorized or directed by the Panel.
"Impasse"means that point in negotiations at which the parties are unable to reach full agreement; provided, however, that they have made earnest efforts to reach agreement by direct negotiations and have used without success voluntary arrangements for settlement.
"Panel"means the Federal Service Impasses Panel or a quorum thereof.
"Party" means the Federal agency, establishment or activity or the labor organization, as defined in sections 2 (a) and (e) of the Order, participating in the negotiation of a labor - management agreement.
"Voluntary arrangements"means those methods adopted by the parties for the purpose of assisting them in their negotiation of a labor agreement, which may include (a) joint factfinding com-

mittees without recommendations; (b) referral to a higher authority within the agency and /or the labor organization; (c) utilization of the services of the Federal Mediation and Conciliation Service or other third-party mediation assistance; or (d) any other method which the parties deem appropriate except third-party factfinding with recommendations, or arbitration unless these methods are expressly authorized or directed by the Panel.

PART 2471 -- PROCEDURES OF THE PANEL

AUTHORITY: The provisions of this Part 2471 issued under 5 U.S.C. 3301, 7301; Executive Order 11491, 34 F.R. 17605, 3 CFR 191, 1969 Comp.

2471.1 Who may initiate.

(a) When an impasse occurs during the course of labor negotiations, either party, or the parties jointly, may request the panel to consider the matter, by filing a request as herein-after provided.

(b) The panel may, upon referral of the Executive Secretary, undertake the consideration of any matter where voluntary ar-rangements have failed and neither party has requested the pan-el's consideration.

2471.2 What to file.

A request to the panel for consideration of an impasse must be in writing and include the following essential information.

(a) Identification of the parties and person(s) authorized to initiate the request;

(b) Statement that an impasse has been reached;

(c) Statement of unresolved issues and the present position(s) of the initiating party or parties with respect to those issues; and

(d) The nature and extent of all voluntary arrangements uti-lized.

2471.3 Request form.

FSIP Form 1 has been prepared for use by the parties in filing a request to the panel for consideration of a negotiation impasse.[1] Copies are available upon request to the Office of the Executive Secretary.

2471.4 Where to file.

Requests to the panel provided for in this part, and inquiries or correspondence on the status of impasses or other related matters, should be directed to the Executive Secretary, Federal Service Impasses Panel, 1900 E. Street N.W., Washington, D.C. 20415.

2471.5 Copies and service.

Concurrently with the submission of a request for panel con-sideration, or when the panel acts of its own motion, a copy of

---

1. Filed as a part of the original document.

such request or panel action shall be served by the party initiating the request or by the panel on the party(ies) to the dispute and on any third party, if utilized.

2471.6 Initial procedures of the panel.

(a) Upon receipt of a request for consideration of an impasse, the panel will review the request and determine whether:

(1) Negotiations should be resumed;

(2) Other voluntary arrangements should be utilized by the parties to help resolve the impasse; or

(3) The panel will proceed under its authority as prescribed in 2471.7-2471.14.

(b) The panel will not process requests whenever it determines that the impasse is based solely on the negotiability of an issue or issues. In such cases, the filing party will be directed to avail itself of the remedies provided for in section 11 (c) of the order. However, when any of the several subjects of the impasse is based on the negotiability of an issue, then such subject(s) shall be referred for handling under section 11 (c) and the balance of the dispute will be considered by the panel.

(c) The parties will be promptly advised in writing of the panel's decision.

2471.7 Use of voluntary factfinding with recommendations, or arbitration.

The parties may resort to voluntary factfinding with recommendations, or arbitration, to resolve an impasse, only when authorized or directed by the panel, and provided they have:

(a) Made a joint request to the panel in writing for such authority;

(b) Agreed on the method of selecting the third party;

(c) Agreed to share the cost of the proceedings; and

(d) Used without success any other voluntary arrangement for settlement.

2471.8 Definition of issue(s); appointment of factfinder(s).

When the panel determines that resolution of an impasse requires factfinding, it will:
(a) Specify the issue(s) to be resolved; and
(b) Appoint a factfinder(s) to conduct the hearing.

2471.9 Notice of hearing.

The notice of hearing will provide at least ten (10) days notice
and shall be served on the parties to the impasse and will include:
(a) The names of the parties to the dispute:
(b) The time, place and nature of the hearing;
(c) The issues to be resolved; and
(d) The name(s) of the factfinder(s) appointed.

2471.10 Authority of factfinder(s).

Factfinders are authorized to:
(a) Administer oaths or affirmations;
(b) Take testimony by deposition;
(c) Require a verbatim report of the proceedings;
(d) Conduct the hearing in open or closed sessions; and
(e) Permit briefs to be filed after the close of a hearing.

2471.11 Availability of hearing transcript.

When a verbatim report of any proceeding is authorized, the
parties will make their own arrangements with the reporter for the
purchase of copies. A copy will be available for inspection by
either party to the proceeding at the office of the Executive Secretary.

2471.12 Report of the factfinder(s) and action by the Panel.

(a) The factfinder(s) shall submit a report to the panel within
a reasonable time, normally not to exceed 30 days, after the close
of the hearing. The parties will be advised when the report has been
transmitted to the panel. The report will include findings on:
(1) The history of the current negotiations, including the initial

positions of the parties, and a report of items agreed to in whole or part ;

(2) The unresolved issues and the efforts made by the parties to reach agreement thereon;

(3) The context within which the negotiations have taken place; and

(4) Any other matters relevant to the impasse.

(b) After receipt of the report of the factfinder(s), the panel will evaluate the impasse and issue its recommendations to the parties for settlement.

2471.13 Duty of each party.

(a) Within a period not to exceed thirty (30) days following receipt of the panel's recommendations for settlement, each party must either:

(1) Accept the panel's recommendations and so notify the Executive Secretary, or

(2) Reach with the other party a settlement of all unresolved issues, and so notify the Executive Secretary; or

(3) Submit a written statement to the panel setting forth its reasons for not accepting the panel's recommendations and reaching a settlement of all unresolved issues.

(b) A reasonable extension of the 30-day period may be authorized by the Executive Secretary for good cause shown when requested in writing by either party prior to the expiration of the 30-day period.

2471.14 Settlement action by the panel.

In the event that there remains any unresolved issues thirty (30) days following issuance of the panel's recommendations, or any extension thereof, the panel, after due consideration of the reports of the parties, will take whatever action it deems necessary to bring the dispute to settlement.

> David T. Roadley,
> Executive Secretary

(F.R. Doc. 70-11131; Filed, Aug. 24, 1970; 8:45 a.m.)

INDEX